CROWOOD SPORTS GUIDES
ORIENTEERING
SKILLS • TECHNIQUES • TRAINING

CROWOOD SPORTS GUIDES
ORIENTEERING
SKILLS • TECHNIQUES • TRAINING

THE CROWOOD PRESS

First published in 2010 by
The Crowood Press Ltd
Ramsbury, Marlborough
Wiltshire SN8 2HR

www.crowood.com

British Library Cataloguing-in-Publication Data
A catalogue record for this book is available from the British Library.

ISBN 978 1 84797 206 4

Disclaimer

The author and the publisher do not accept any responsibility in any manner whatsoever
for any error or omission, or any loss, damage, injury, adverse outcome, or liability of any
kind incurred as a result of the use of any of the information contained in this book, or
reliance upon it. If in doubt about any aspect of orienteering, readers are advised to seek
professional advice. Since the exercises and other physical activities described in this book
may be too strenuous in nature for some readers to engage in safely, it is essential that a
doctor is consulted before undertaking such exercises and activities.

Typefaces used: Gill Sans Light (main text); Gill Sans and Gill Sans Bold (headings).

Typeset and designed by
D & N Publishing
Baydon, Wiltshire.

Printed and bound in Malaysia by Times Offset (M) Sdn Bhd.

CONTENTS

ACKNOWLEDGEMENTS

The Author (and publishers) would like to thank all the orienteers in the photographs and especially the following for their help and cooperation in the production of this book:

Iain Smith-Ward for technical advice and j-pegging all the maps.

Liz Campbell, Duncan Archer, Pippa Whitehouse and Richard Lecky Thompson for reading and helping me to make it all up to date.

Julian Donelly for help with the periodization chart technology.

Graham Gristwood and Pippa Whitehouse for their race commentaries.

Martin Bagness/Warrior OC (WAROC) for the drawings in Chapter 14.

Lakeland Orienteering Club, Warrior Orienteering Club, South Ribble Orienteering Club and the North West Orienteering Association for use of their maps.

Áron Less, Secretary General of the World Orienteering Championships 2009 for the sprint and long race final maps and courses.

Unless otherwise stated, the photographs in this book were taken by Phil Burdge.

PART I

INTRODUCTION

CHAPTER 1

INTRODUCTION TO ORIENTEERING

Orienteering is a running sport. The competitive orienteer runs with a map and compass, choosing routes, to find a fixed number of control points that are marked precisely on the map and indicated in the terrain by large red and white control markers, or 'kites'. Each control point has a code number and a means to register each visit. This is usually an electronic box, but it could be a pin punch or letters to record. The course will vary in length and difficulty depending upon the age, experience and fitness of the competitor. Within each class, it is the person finding all the controls in the right order in the shortest time who wins.

A control point with a code number and electronic box to register each visit.

History

The sport of orienteering was pioneered in Sweden. Major Ernst Killander organized one of the first official events in 1918 as a result of his concern for a falling interest in athletics and a lack of use of the forest environment. It has grown since then to become one of the most popular sports in Sweden. From Sweden, the sport spread to the rest of Scandinavia and then to Europe, followed by other countries throughout the world.

It was a Swede, Baron 'Rak' Lagerfelt of the Stockholm Orienteering Club, who had a major influence in establishing the sport in Britain. In 1962, Lagerfelt came to Scotland to help develop the sport. His work culminated in the first championship being held in May 1962 at Dunkeld and the formation of the Scottish Orienteering Association.

The first orienteering clubs were formed by athletes with an interest in navigation, climbing and fell running. Southern Navigators, South Ribble Orienteering Club and Edinburgh Southern Orienteering Club were the first of the many clubs that now cover the whole of the United Kingdom. The interest and organizational energy of well-established and international athletes such as John Disley, Chris Brasher, Bruce Tulloch, Martin Hyman and Gordon Pirie helped a great deal in developing the sport in its early days, including the implementation of guidelines and rules of competition.

In 1967 the English and Scottish Orienteering Associations amalgamated to form the British Orienteering Federation. The BOF is the governing body of the sport, which co-ordinates the administration and maintenance of standards.

Maps

The growth of the sport has largely been influenced by the improvement in the quality of maps. The early events were dependent upon copies of Ordnance Survey maps. Now, with advances in printing technology, all events provide a specially drawn large-scale coloured map for each competitor.

Look at the map and see if you can spot differences with other maps you use.

The areas are surveyed and the map digitally drawn by orienteers using international specifications for orienteering maps. Contours of 5m or 2.5m show the precise nature of the terrain and other details, such as large boulders, pits, gullies, depressions and small crags that enable the orienteer to know exactly where he or she is at all times, as well as providing a large number of potential control sites. The time-consuming job of making orienteering maps involving photogrammetry, surveying and cartography, and the printing is done by one of the small businesses that offer this specialist service. Many clubs are also able to draw on the skills of members who have made map-making their spare-time interest.

A World-Wide Sport

The International Orienteering Federation is the umbrella organization for the four recognized orienteering disciplines: Foot O, Mountain Bike O, Ski O and Trail O. It was founded in 1961 and aims to promote the development of orienteering in its member countries. Most events held in these countries are open to all standards of competitors, including beginners. The IOF also creates and

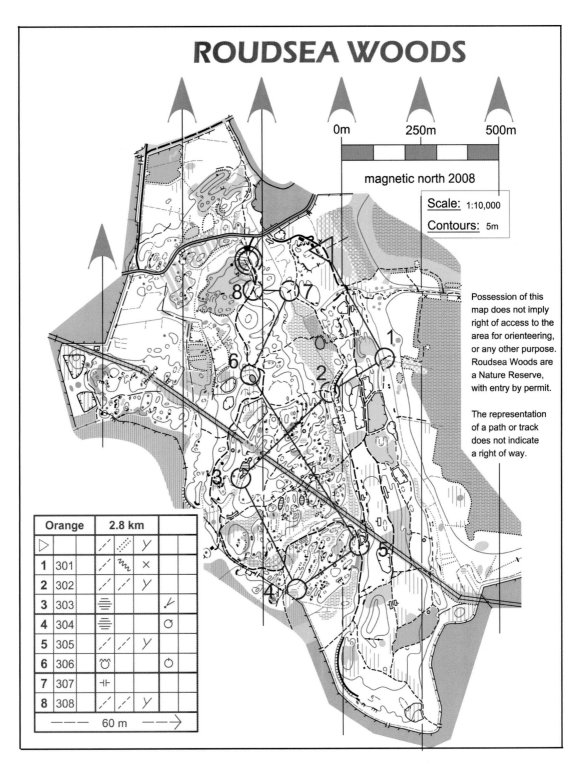

ROUDSEA WOODS

0m   250m   500m

magnetic north 2008

Scale: 1:10,000

Contours: 5m

Possession of this map does not imply right of access to the area for orienteering, or any other purpose. Roudsea Woods are a Nature Reserve, with entry by permit.

The representation of a path or track does not indicate a right of way.

Orange		2.8 km			
▷					
1	301				
2	302				
3	303				
4	304				
5	305				
6	306				
7	307				
8	308				
——— 60 m ——→					

An orienteering map with an Orange (TD3) course.

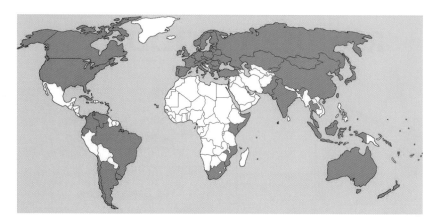

The International Orienteering Federation has more than seventy member countries.

maintains a world event programme including World Championships for seniors, students, juniors and veterans.

Types of Orienteering

At its most competitive, the sport of orienteering, or 'foot O', offers a lot to the athlete who likes to think, as well as run. The sport is organized to offer an adventurous challenge to children and adults of all ages and athletic ability. String courses for the under tens allow even three- or four-year-old children to enjoy finding controls while running through woodland.

Events cater for all ages and abilities.

MTBO. Mountain bike orienteering is just like foot O using specially drawn maps. (Bryan Singleton/GB MBO Team)

String courses allow very young children to enjoy finding controls while running through woodland.

Events cater for all ages and abilities, giving an opportunity for athletes and non-athletes alike to participate in a running sport at whatever level is appropriate for them. Walking round a course while employing accurate map reading may not put you at the top of your class, but it certainly will not put you at the bottom. The story of the tortoise and the hare can be aptly applied to this sport.

OTHER FORMS OF ORIENTEERING POPULAR THROUGHOUT THE WORLD

Long O – at least double your normal distance.
Sprint O – very short and very fast.
Night O – all types of orienteering can be held in the dark.
Trail O – orienteering adapted for those with disabilities. The challenge is to identify a control site from several possible kites seen from a station on a path. Points are gained from correct identification and occasionally the time it takes to make a decision.
Ski O – cross-country skiing with a special map and marked trails
MBO – a Mountain Bike Orienteering Event is like foot O, where each competitor visits controls in a set order. They use a specially drawn, large-scale, orienteering-style map, drawn to international MBO standards. Mountain Bike Orienteering Score Events use orienteering-style maps, or suitably modified Ordnance Survey maps.
Horse O – Le Trec; navigation on horseback.

Orienteering gives you confidence in handling a map and compass in any navigational situation, whether it is negotiating your local footpaths or exploring wilderness areas on the other side of the world. It will take you into some our most attractive woodland, forest, heath and moorland, many of which are not normally accessible to the public.

Orienteering takes you into many different types of terrain.

CHAPTER 2

GETTING STARTED

The best way to start is to go to a local orienteering event. There are orienteering events held on every weekend of the year all over the country, usually on a Sunday morning. Find out which is your nearest club by going on the British Orienteering website (see Useful Contacts), then consult your local club's fixture list. There will be courses for the whole range of age and abilities, so whether you are familiar with maps or not, there will be a course suitable for you.

Clothing and Equipment

For your first event just go along with comfortable clothes you can run in and don't mind getting muddy. Leg cover is compulsory unless otherwise stated. Take a light waterproof jacket or cagoule for poor weather. Wear walking or running shoes with a good grip.

Wear clothes you don't mind getting muddy. Regular orienteers wear a light nylon suit and studded shoes.

EQUIPMENT FOR FIRST EVENT

The following equipment should be gathered together for your first event:

- safety whistle pinned in a pocket out of the way
- safety pins to fasten the control descriptions and control card if you are given one
- compass
- red pen in case you have to copy control points or map corrections
- clear polythene A4 bag to protect the map
- insulation tape to wrap round your laces to stop them coming undone
- money for the entry fee.

All you need to go orienteering. A lightweight top, studded shoes, a compass and an electronic dibber, which can be hired.

Colour-Coded Courses

At nearly all events you will be able to choose from a number of colour-coded courses. These have a universal standard of distance and difficulty. Some events will offer extra colours such as Red, a TD3 longer than Orange or Black, a TD5 longer than Brown. You might also find that events have age group classes as well but stick to EOD – enter on the day – colour courses to start with.

Colour-Coded Courses

Technical difficulty: TD1 – easy; TD5 – hard.

White courses are for six- to ten-year olds.

White (TD1) White courses are very easy with just about all controls on paths. They are mainly used by six- to ten-year olds and family groups. Length of course: 1.0–1.5km. This will take between 15–30min.

Yellow (TD2) Yellow courses use simple linear features like tracks, paths, walls and streams with one obvious route between control points. They are mainly used by under twelves and families. Length of course: 1.5–2.5km. This will usually take 20–40min.

Orange (TD3) Orange courses offer route choice and require basic use of the compass. They are ideal to start with if you are familiar with maps. Length of course: 2.5–3.5km. Expect to be out for 50–60min when you first start.

Light Green (TD4) Light Green courses are ideal for improvers. The technical difficulty begins to increase with more route choice and controls on small features. Length of course: 2.5–3.5km. This will take 33–55min for most finishers.

Green (TD5) Green courses are technically difficult and use contour and point features. Applications of advanced techniques are necessary to complete a course efficiently. They are used mostly by those wanting a short but challenging course. Length of course: 3.5–5km, likely duration 35–55min.

Blue (TD5) Blue courses are technically difficult. They are longer and more physically challenging than the Green. This type of course attracts experienced orienteers. Length of course: 5–7.5km, likely duration 50–70min.

Brown (TD5) Brown courses are physically demanding and technically difficult. They are designed to challenge experienced orienteers. Length of course: 7.5–10km. This will take 60–85min for most finishers.

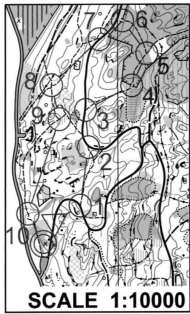

SCALE 1:10000

WHITE , Length 1.4 km

Start		forest road
1.	101	forest road - path junction
2.	102	forest road - path junction
3.	103	forest road - path junction
4.	104	gate
5.	105	path junction
6.	106	gate
7.	107	forest road - path junction
8.	108	path junction
9.	109	path junction
10.	110	path - stream junction

90 m from last control to finish. No tapes

A TD1 White course with written descriptions.

At some small events you may come across the traditional control card and pin-punch recording system.

Registration

When you arrive at the event, go to the registration or enquiries and ask for help if you think you need it. There is usually a list of courses on display to help you choose. If this is your first event, try the Yellow or Orange. These courses are straight-forward and will give you a taste of the sport and the procedures required to complete a course.

Having decided which course you want to do, you may have to complete a card with your details or sign a list so that the organizer knows you will be out in the area. Once you have paid the entry fee, you will be given a map if you have to mark your own course on it, otherwise a pre-marked map will be provided at the start. If you are doing the White or Yellow course, the pre-marked map will be provided at registration. Take a control description list and hire an electronic card or collect a control card if the event is non-electronic. If you are given a start time, check you will have at least 30min to get ready and arrive at the start.

Electronic Cards

The modern way of recording that you have been to every control point in the right order is with an electronic card. You 'punch' or 'dib' at the start, at each control and the finish. This system will also give you 'splits', showing how long you took to get to each control point as well as your total time. At each event there is always a 'clear' station to delete any information stored and not wanted.

Control Descriptions

Control descriptions tell you what you are looking for and the code number to be found at each control. There will be many other controls in the area, as well as the ones on your course. There are two types of control descriptions: written or pictorial. If you are given a pictorial list, spend some time checking that you know what feature each control is on. If you are

An electronic card – a SPORTident (SI) dibber.

An Emit Brick – another electronic card. These two types of electronic cards are used to register your arrival at each control.

unsure just ask for help, which will be willingly given. Refer to 'Appendix: International Control Description Symbols' to see exactly how they are laid out.

The control descriptions will be on every pre-marked map, but it is better to have a separate list as well, which can be attached to a wrist band or a sleeve. This enables you to read the features you are looking for with the control codes without having to unfold your map.

The Map

The map is especially drawn for orienteering with its own international legend and lines drawn to magnetic north to simplify using the compass. Study the map to see if there are any unusual features and check the scale. Orienteers get used to using maps of different scales, with the most popular being 1:10,000. Other scales commonly used are 1:15,000, 1:7,500 and 1:5,000. Some compasses have exchangeable scale strips used for measuring and which can be slid on or off the front edge. If you have chosen to do a White or Yellow course and receive the

An orienteer with a specially designed description list holder attached to his wrist.

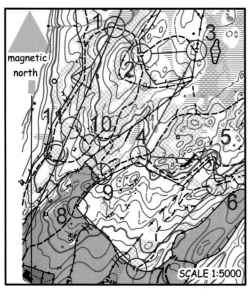

YELLOW, Length 2.0 km
Start
1.	201	path - pylon line crossing
2.	202	gate
3.	203	gate
4.	205	path junction
5.	206	crossing point in wall
6.	207	path
7.	208	gate
8.	209	wall bend
9.	210	path - stream crossing
10.	211	path - old wall junction
11.	212	pylon

90 m from last control to finish.

A TD2 Yellow course, mainly for under twelves and families. The triangle marks the start.

map at registration, there will be time to study the map and course before you start.

When orienteering, everything should be attached to you except the map. The map needs to be given your full attention. Get yourself ready, then make your way to the start.

Ready to Go

Start

When you arrive at the start, have a look at how the system works. You should find there are pre-marked maps on waterproof paper, or protected in a sealed polythene bag. These will be in course-labelled boxes set up at the start. Competitors are set off at 1-minute intervals, with only one person on each

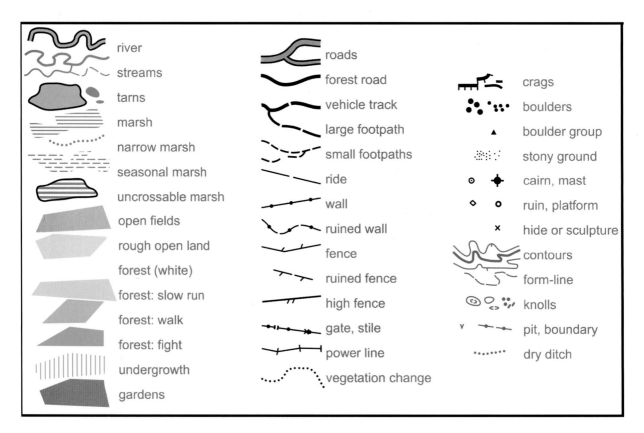

A universal orienteering map legend.

course starting at a time. If you attend a large event and pre-enter into your age class, you will be given a start time, which must be kept to. At a local event, you will be able to start as soon as your chosen course is free. Pick up your map and you are ready to go.

If you find it is necessary to copy your course from a master map do this carefully, double-checking that the centre of each hand-drawn control circle on your map matches the centre of each circle on the master map. Draw the circle so that you can see the map detail within it.

The Course

The triangle on the map is the start kite. This may be a short distance from the actual start line. Follow the marked route to this point. It is normally on a clearly defined feature such as a path junction. Set the map with your compass and decide which route you want to take to find the first control. Is there more than one route that you could take? What sort of features can you follow so that you keep map contact and not get lost? Having made these decisions, off you go.

Controls

Each control is a three-dimensional red and white triangular kite. It will have an identification code number, which should correspond with the ones on your description list. Always check the code before you punch, as you might have found a control on a different course! However, if you punch any wrong controls you won't be disqualified so long as you eventually find all the right controls in the correct order.

Finish

What joy! You have found all the controls and completed your course. The finish is indicated by the double circle on the map. Find the download point where you register your card and get a print-out of

An orienteer registering at a control with an electronic dibber.

your time and all your splits. If you have an 'mp', or mispunch, it means you went to a wrong control, or missed one out, and are, unfortunately, disqualified.

Results

Very soon a list will go up to show the results of everyone who has finished each course in time order. If there isn't this facility, you will have to wait until the results are put up on the organizing club's web page.

Analysis

How did you get on? Your first goal is to find all the controls. To start to improve your orienteering skills, after the race draw your route on the map, including all the unintended diversions. Compare your

---

TOP TIPS

- Keep the map oriented all the time. The features on the map should always match the features on the ground.
- Fold the map up so that it is easier to see where you are.
- 'Thumb' the map, by keeping your thumb on your last known position. This helps in reading the map while on the move and makes it easier to focus on a particular section of the map.
- Always check the code number at each control.

---

split times and routes with others and spot which legs you could have completed in a faster time. What went wrong? You will find more about event analysis in Chapter 7.

Permanent Courses

A permanent course is a fixed course available for anyone to try out or practise orienteering on at any time of the year. They are usually designed for beginners, families and school groups, but often include options for more experienced orienteers. Map packs include descriptions and a variety of course options. To find out where the nearest permanent courses are, contact your local club or look on the British Orienteering website.

Families can enjoy orienteering on permanent courses as well as going to events. (Ian Smith-Ward)

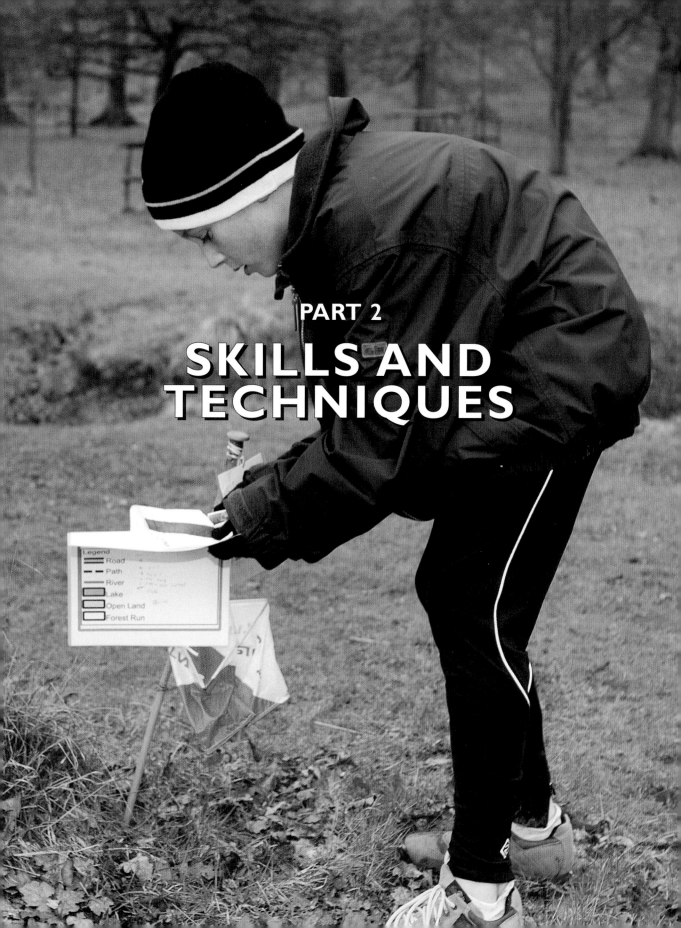

PART 2

SKILLS AND TECHNIQUES

CHAPTER 3

BASIC TECHNIQUES

White (TD1)

- Knowing the basic map legend of colours, paths, tracks and buildings.
- Understanding basic map orientation using features, or the sun or a simple compass.
- Following a route along paths and tracks.
- Finding the controls at every decision point.
- Folding then thumbing the map.
- Using the paths and line features as 'handrails'.

Yellow (TD2)

- Learning more legend, for example line features to follow as handrails, such as tracks, paths, walls, fences, streams.
- Understanding features next to line features, which may be used as control points, or be used to check progress, such as ponds, large marshes or big crags.
- Selecting then following the one obvious route, with one or two decision points to be made at junctions without controls to help.
- Simple distance judgement and relocation skills.

Orange (TD3)

- Route choices to be made using a variety of handrails.
- Using the compass to cut corners by aiming off.
- Route simplification using attack points.
- Using distance judgement.
- Orienteering over short distances without handrails, using catching features.

The Skills and Techniques Required for White, Yellow and Orange Courses

Now we will look at the techniques needed to complete and enjoy your first experiences of competitive orienteering at Technical Difficulty (TD) 1, TD2 and TD3. If you are a parent whose child would like to go orienteering, read through the White and Yellow sections together then discuss the tactics and strategies suggested. If you can read a map already, or want to keep one step ahead of your children, start with Orange, you'll be fine.

TD1 White

First, let's look at what is needed to complete a White course.

White course control 3. Hold the map so that you are looking along the route you want to take. All the features on the map should match the corresponding features on the ground.

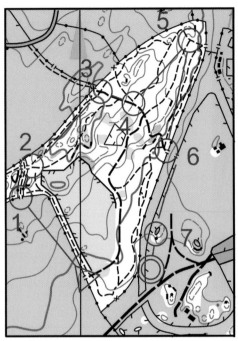

Course WHITE, Length 1.1 km

Start		Gateway
1.	101	Gateway
2.	102	Path junction
3.	103	Path junction
4.	104	Path junction
5.	105	Path junction
6.	106	Gateway
7.	107	Fenced enclosure. South end

70 m from last control to finish. No tapes

WHITE		1.1 km		
▷				
1	101	⊣⊢		
2	102	⁄⁄	⁄⁄	Y
3	103	⁄⁄	⁄⁄	Y
4	104	⁄⁄	⁄⁄	Y
5	105	⁄⁄	⁄⁄	Y
6	106	⊣⊢		
7	107	⌂		Y
○<		70 m		>○

A White course with written and pictorial descriptions.

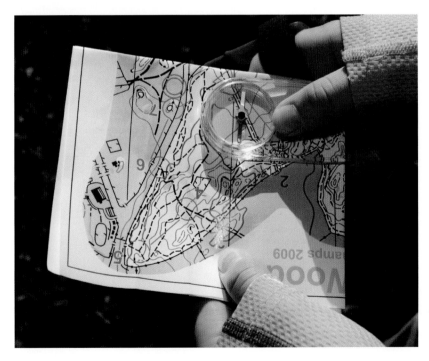

The map is set at control 3 using a clip compass. The compass needle is in line with the North lines on the map.

Legend

Can you identify the main features on the map? Check against the map legend in Chapter 2. Imagine you are doing this course – what features will you follow and will it be wooded or open on either side of you? What features are used for control sites?

Setting, or Orienting, the Map

This is the most important technique you will need in order to orienteer. It means holding the map so that you are looking along the route you want to take whilst the map is set to north. All the features on the map match the corresponding features on the ground. If the map is set, it is easy to see whether to run straight, or turn left or right.

Look at the White course. You will follow paths nearly all the way round the course. At control 3, will you turn left or right to find control 4? At control 4 you have three choices. If the map is set you will easily see which path to take.

Folding the Map

The map is much easier to hold and read if it is folded so that you are just looking at the section where you are. For young beginners it is helpful if, at the start, an older person folds the map square to the sides with just the course and a north arrow showing.

Thumbing the Map

To help you run and still keep the map set, get used to holding the map with your thumb beside your last known position.

Compass

It is recommended that a compass is introduced at the very beginning. At White and Yellow stages a clip compass or a 'micro-racer' thumb compass can be used

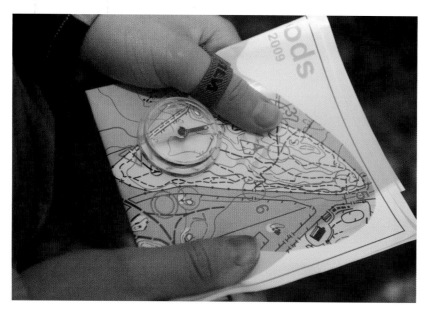

to set the map simply. Whatever sort of compass you have, the red end of the compass needle should point to the north (top) of the map all the time. Clip the clip compass to one side of the map or, if a micro-racer is used, hold the map in the compass hand. Hold the map so that you are looking along the route you want to take. Turn your body until the compass needle is in line with the north lines on the map. Don't forget that you always hold the map so that you are looking along the route you want to take.

Control 4. The map is set using a micro racer compass. Don't forget that you always hold the map so that you are looking along the route you want to take.

TIP

Try to imagine where you are going, rather than where you are. If you are following the path from control 2 to control 3, where are you going? Answer: you are going to the next path junction – look ahead and look out for it.

Yellow courses are used by under-twelves and newcomers without any map-reading experience. (Ian Smith-Ward)

Practice task Make a miniature Treasure Island then draw a map of it. Use a rope or washing line to make the outline, add pot plants for trees, a bowl of water for a lake, something larger such as a chair or step ladder for a lookout point and any other features that will fit on the ground and in your imagination. Try to make it big enough to walk through with your map. Draw your map, then bury some treasure, mark it on your map and see if someone else can find it. Have fun!

TD2 Yellow

Can you spot the differences between the routes you follow on the White course and this Yellow course?

What new features will you follow and need to know to find the controls? Refer to the legend in Chapter 2. Are there any new control sites? When will you have to make major decisions?

Choosing a Route

There will always be one obvious route, but *you* have to spot it and tell yourself what features you will need to follow before you set out from each control. What line feature will you choose to follow from control 3 to 4? Which three features would you follow between controls 8 and 9?

Checking Off Features

You are now a navigator. Keep reading the map. Look out for features coming up on the map and check them off as you pass them. If you see a distinct feature along your route, find it on your map and check it off. Try to keep your thumb close to where you are as you check off the features, as this will help you to know where you are at all times. Imagine you are going from control 8 to control 9. What features will you see on your left to check off your progress?

Distance Judgement – Knowing When to Look and Turn

If you are running the leg from control 1 to control 2, how will you know when to pick up the path? Look for when the path bends. Will the junction be on your left or right and how far? Start to get into the habit of getting the feel of how far you

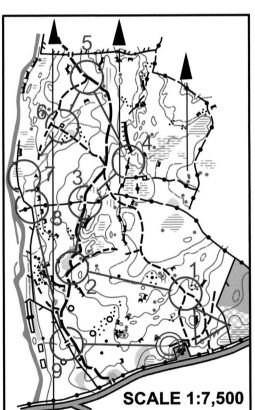

YELLOW, Length 1.4 km
Start
1. 154 path junction
2. 157 path junction
3. 155 old wall junction
4. 156 wall stream crossing
5. 159 path junction
6. 160 ruin, south west side
7. 163 stream bend
8. 164 wall, fence crossing
9. 165 gate
190 m from last control to finish.

YELLOW	1.4 km			
▷				
1	154	⁄⁄	⁄⁄	Y
2	157	⁄⁄	⁄⁄	Y
3	155	⁄⁄	⁄⁄	Y
4	156	⁄⁄	∿	X
5	159	⁄⁄	⁄⁄	Y
6	160	⬚		⌓
7	163	∿		<
8	164	⁄⁄	⌅	X
9	165	⊣⊢		
◯✕		190 m		✕◯

A Yellow course. The controls are in the centre of each circle and the red lines linking each circle are to help you to see where the next control is.

If you see distinct features along your route, find them on your map and check them off.

have gone. Look at leg 3 to 4 again. The wall junction is about halfway. On leg 5 to 6 the path bends about halfway to the path junction where you need to turn to find the ruin. Will the ruin be on your left or right? Concentrating on your route all the time will also help you to keep track of how far you have gone.

Getting Lost … and Finding Out Where you Are

Where would all the fun be if you didn't get lost and have an adventure? Finding out where you are is called relocation. Most orienteers, however experienced they are, frequently get lost and have to relocate. It's not as scary as you might think.

Imagine you were going between control 1 and control 2 and missed the turn-off. You might realize this when you reached the wall or next path junction, or you could have run on and ignored everything until you came to control 5. How would you know it was control 5? If you can't work out where you are straight away, stop and think. Don't

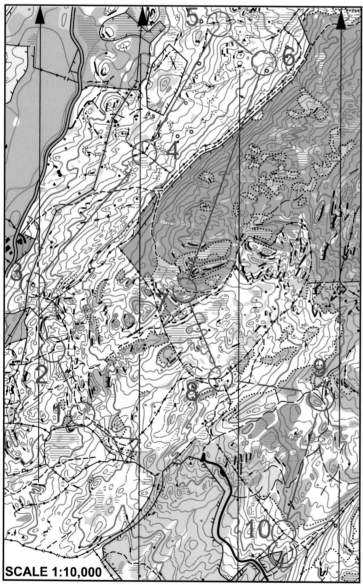

SCALE 1:10,000

An Orange course (TD3). Can you spot the route choices to be made between controls?

ORANGE		2.9 km			
▷					
1	301	⁄′	ⁿₘ	✕	
2	302	⁄			⟨
3	303	⊏ ⊐			○
4	304	⁄	⋀	⅄	
5	305	ⁿₘ	⁑	⅄	
6	306	ⁿₘ			⟨
7	307	⁄′			⊢
8	308	⁄	⋀	⅄	
9	310	⁝	⁝	⅄	
10	311	⁄	⁄	⅄	
✕		50 m			✕○

TD3 ORANGE TECHNIQUES TOOLBOX

Techniques for TD3 Orange:

- plan your route backwards
- use handrails for route choice
- use attack points for finding controls
- check the map scale for measuring distance
- use pacing for distance estimation
- know the basic contour features
- understand basic compass use
- use the compass for cutting corners and aiming off
- look out for catching features
- have a relocation plan.

> **TIP**
>
> Remember that every feature used for a control is at the very centre of each control circle on the map.

worry. Look around you – what can you see that is very distinctive? Can you work out what you have done? You can decide to retrace your steps to the last control, or to a point where you knew where you were. If you are completely stuck, ask for help, which will generally be willingly given. Ask someone who looks friendly and willing to stop and, if you prefer, get them to show you how to reach the finish.

Practice task Draw a map of a room in your house, then hide some 'treasures' and mark these on your map for someone to find.

TD3 Orange

Orange courses give you a real taste of orienteering whilst you master the basic techniques. If you have done lots of Yellow courses and can keep the map set with a compass, now is the time to move on to Orange.

Route Choice

Have a close look at the Orange course. It should be noticeable that there are route options between most controls. TD3 is all about choosing a route then following it. If you want to orienteer efficiently it is advisable to have a 'toolbox' of techniques into which you can dip. This enables you to develop your own route choice strategies and to follow your chosen route accurately. Don't try them all at once. Select a couple, read through the sections with an orienteering map, visualize yourself doing them, then apply them as soon as there is an opportunity at an event.

Planning your Route Backwards

The best way to plan your route is to look at the control that you are heading for (on the map) and work out your route backwards. Which is the best handrail to lead you into the control? Will you need an attack point to help you to find the control and, if so, can you see one on the map close to the control circle?

Have a look at leg 2 to 3. It is short but quite complex map reading. Control 3 is a ruin. What line feature is closest? The pylon line. So which is the easiest route to the pylon line?

Handrails. The marshes, steep slope and the line of crags can all be used as handrails to find control 5.

Handrails

'Which way shall I go?' Look at the leg between controls 3 and 4. There are a few choices. Which routes are the safest? Following line features as handrails is safe and often very fast because you can 'hang on' to them. The safest route would be to keep under the pylons, then pick up the path where it crosses the pylons, follow it to the wall by the green, then follow the wall round to the control.

In the example shown here, long lines of crags, a long linear marsh, the edge of a steep slope and a long valley are examples of non-line features that can also be used as handrails.

Attack Points

An attack point is used to help find a control. If a control is on an isolated feature, such as a clearing, marsh, hilltop or ruin, plan your route using handrails with an attack point. The attack point is a distinct point on a handrail close to the

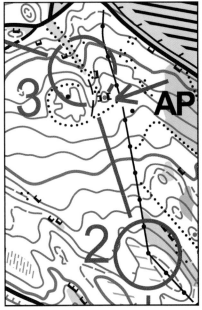

Attack points. Plan your route from the attack point, which would be the hill with crags close to the wall.

control. It needs to be easy to find, so that you can run as fast as you want to get there. Choose your attack point first, then plan your route. Once you reach the

attack point, it is wise to slow right down while you double your concentration, setting and reading the map carefully until you see the feature you are looking for and the control. A compass bearing and pace counting are often recommended to find a control from an attack point.

Map Scales

It is important to know the scale of the map so that you can estimate or measure the distance between features.

For example, on leg 7 to 8 on the Orange course you may decide to go straight across the open woodland to find the wall junction. How far is it? Use a ruler to measure and refer to the scale table to find the answer.

Most compasses have a centimetre

Map Scale	1mm on map =	10mm/1cm on map =
1:5,000	5m	50m
1:7,500	7.5m	75m
1:10,000	10m	100m
1:15,000	15m	150m

scale on the front or side edge. This can be used to measure distance accurately from the map.

Distance Estimation

If you have an up-to-date map with lots of detail and distinctive land shapes this should make checking off your progress straightforward, whatever the scale of map. With a few years of experience you will start to get the feel of how much ground you have covered over different types of terrain. However, this method is only guesswork and you may find it is not very reliable, especially over rough ground or in forest with low visibility.

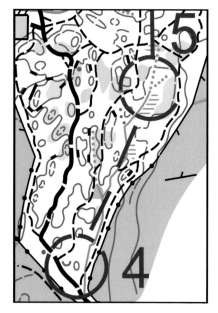

Attack points. The path bend is a good attack point as it is close to the control, so the left-hand path would be safer.

1:5,000 scale. Always know the scale of the map so that you can estimate or measure distances.

1:7,500 scale.

1:10,000 scale.

1:15,000 scale.

One way of structuring checking off the distance covered is to divide the leg or part of the leg into fractions or sections; you then work on comparing and matching the 'feel' of it, or the time it takes. For example, you are cutting across a block of forest looking out for a path. There is a wall to pass halfway. Once you come to the wall, you know you have to travel the same distance again to reach the path.

Look at the Orange course legs 4 to 5 and 5 to 6. The distance to the first fence corner is a bit less than the length of the fence, but similar to the section from the far fence corner to the stream. The distance from control 5 to control 6 is the same length as the fence. You would allow longer getting to control 6 because it is uphill.

To be more accurate, the orienteer knows how many double paces he or she takes to 100m. Then, having measured the distance from the map, a quick calculation is made and the number of double paces needed counted out.

Pacing

To calculate your paces for 100m mark out a measured stretch of track or path and run the distance, counting every alternate step, that is every time your right or left foot hits the ground. Keep the stride length even. Do not run too fast; start again if you lose count. Do this a few times to give you an average figure. Repeat this procedure at a walk. Now, using a map, measure off some sections between 50 and 200m, then go out to test out your new pace counts. The most useful figure is a walking pace which is the same in any sort of terrain, whether it is flat and easy to move through or hilly and rough. If you miss a control point on the run, relocate and walk in counting paces.

Pacing up to 200m can be very accurate and helps you to know when to look out for the control or feature you are heading for. Pacing over longer distances becomes less reliable, but can be useful back-up information if you lose map contact.

If the control you are heading for is small, such as in a depression or pit, look out for other features nearby that will make the control easier to find – this makes the control larger and your pacing

Pacing 2. Several paths in this area are indistinct, which means you can easily cross them without noticing. Whichever route you take, pace from path to path to be sure you reach the one you want.

TIP

Always link pace counting with reading the map.

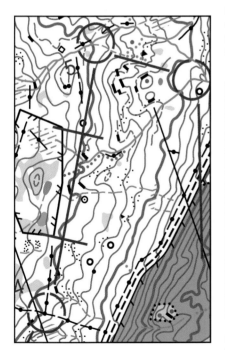

Distance estimation. One way to check off distance is to divide a leg into sections.

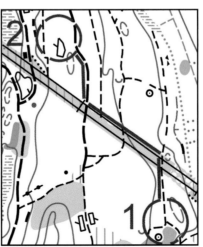

Pacing 1. To find the fenced enclosure it would be easy to turn along the wrong path and miss it. Pace count along the pylon line to be certain of finding the right path as your attack point.

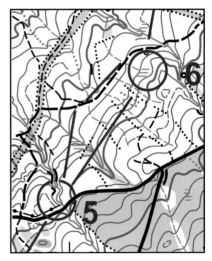

Pacing 3. Whichever route you take to control 6, you will need to pace to be certain of finding the right stream.

will be helpful as a back-up. A pit on its own requires a more accurate count.

The main problem with pacing is remembering the count at the same time as reading the map and checking off features in the terrain. Like any new technique, it needs lots of practice until it becomes familiar. So even if you find it difficult, persevere with your practice because you never know when it will be vital in finding a control.

Contours

Contours are brown lines on the map that indicate the shape and steepness of the ground. Understanding contours is the key to good navigation and is essential if you are going to become a successful orienteer.

At TD3 Orange you will need to become familiar with basic contour principles. Have another look at the Orange course; you can complete the course without knowing about contours, but because they provide more

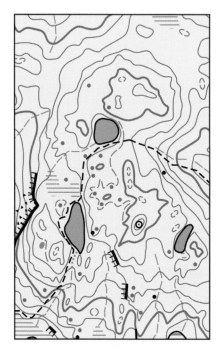

An area where an understanding of contours will enable you to navigate through it. Contours show the shape and steepness of the ground.

information about the steepness and shape of the ground they help you to keep better track of where you are and cut corners confidently.

Look at this map, which is full of contour lines. The more contours there are, the higher the ground. Which is the highest point and what would you find there? The closer the contours, the steeper the ground. Where are the steepest parts? Where is it flat? There are many small hills shown by ring contours. How many can you count? The heavier brown lines are index contours drawn every 25m (five contours). These help to show how much climbing you will have to do on a route choice.

The broken blue lines are minor streams that flow down small valleys called re-entrants. Look at the way the contours bend to show the re-entrants. Can you find the re-entrants without a stream in them? The broken contour lines are called form lines; they are drawn to show the orienteer changes in the shape of the ground that cannot be shown by the regular 5m contour.

Contours. Each contour is represented by a layer on this model. The highest point is seven layers high. (Julian Donnelly)

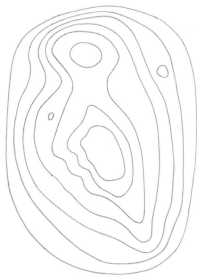

Contour model map. This is how the contours will look on a map showing the height, shape and steepness of the ground. The highest hill is seven contours high.

UNDERSTANDING CONTOURS

- A contour line joins points of equal height.
- Contours show the shape and steepness of the ground.
- The more contours there are, the higher the ground.
- The closer the contours, the steeper the ground.
- No contours means flat ground.
- Index contours are shown by heavier brown lines.
- Ring contours show hilltops.
- Re-entrants are shown by one or more contour lines.
- Broken contours are form lines.

Now look at the path which crosses the area. If you were following the path, where would you go uphill and where would you go down hill? Which is the steepest part of the path and what will you see on the way?

There is more about contours in the next chapter.

Basic Compass Techniques

Orienteering is a map and compass sport, so learn how to use a compass from the outset. Young beginners running White and Yellow courses should choose between a clip compass and a Silva micro-racer thumb compass, both of which can be seen in Chapter 2. They have a clear magnetic needle, which can be used easily for setting the map. For Orange courses and above, you will need to choose between a protractor compass and a thumb compass so that you can cut through the terrain on an accurate line or bearing.

A protractor compass is most commonly used. Choose one that fits neatly in the palm of your hand. You should be able to turn the housing easily; ensure that the magnetic needle settles quickly. An exchangeable map-measuring scale is good to have on the front edge. A long base plate gives you a good line of travel to sight along, but make sure it isn't too big for your hand. Use some cord to attach the compass to your wrist so that it is easy to hold in your hand and doesn't finish up by your knees if you drop it. Do not wear it round your neck with the risk

TIP

Look after your compass – keep it clean and store away from metal objects that may affect the magnetic needle.

Protractor compasses. Choose a compass that fits neatly in the palm of your hand with the loop round your wrist.

of catching it on tree branches and don't tie your whistle to it unless you want a jangle accompaniment while running.

Orienteers may also choose to use a thumb compass. These help in keeping the map set correctly as the compass is held on the map all the time. A lot of practice is needed to use one well, especially when cutting through low visibility terrain.

Setting the Map with a Compass

Orienteering maps always have magnetic north lines marked on them. When these are parallel to the magnetic needle in the compass, you know the map is accurately set. Whenever you want to check that your map is set, hold your compass close to, or on the map, then look at the needle. The red north end should be pointing the same way as the north lines on the map. If not, then turn yourself with the map until the red needle is the same way as the north lines on the map.

If you find it comfortable, you can run with the compass on the map all the time. This is similar to using a thumb compass. You can check constantly that the map is set by keeping an eye on the needle. If you prefer being able to see all of the map without blocking out a bit with the compass, carry your compass in the other hand. It is your choice whether you hold the compass in the same hand or the opposite hand to the map. Look at the photographs in this book and spot the variety of compasses and in which hand they are held.

Taking a Compass Bearing

Taking a bearing from the map is the most accurate way of finding the direction you want to take. Following the compass and checking off features along your route is a technique you will need to progress to at TD4 and TD5. You should feel pleased

A thumb compass will help you keep the map set correctly as the compass is held on the map all the time.

with yourself when you can do this. At TD3 you can use it for cutting corners and aiming off (see next section). The sequence of photos shows how to take a compass bearing.

When taking a compass bearing, the compass is used as a protractor measuring the angle of the direction you want to travel, using north as zero. Knowing that magnetic north is zero, it is then possible to pinpoint any direction you want by measuring the angle.

TIP

Always take an accurate bearing, even if you only use the direction as a rough guide.

To check that your map is set, hold your compass on the map then look at the needle. The red north end should be pointing the same way as the north lines on the map.

Taking a bearing 1. Place a long compass edge on the map along the route line you want to go.

Taking a bearing 2. Hold the base plate firmly on the map while you turn the dial until the north ('N') on the dial points to map north. The lines in the compass housing should be parallel to the N/S lines on the map. Ignore the needle.

Taking a bearing 3. Take the compass off the map. Hold it flat with the direction of travel arrow pointing straight in front of you.

Taking a bearing 4. Turn your body with map and compass together until the needle lies along the north–south line in the housing.

The compass is essential for fast and efficient orienteering, but it should only function as a back-up to your map reading. The controls are found by choosing a rьoute and reading the map, with the compass helping to keep you to your chosen route.

Cutting Corners with the Compass and Aiming Off

There is often a chance to cut through from one line feature to another. Keep the map set and judge the angle you need to run through the woodland or take a bearing across the corner.

If a control or attack point is on a line feature and you have the chance of cutting through to it, it is faster and safer to aim deliberately to one side, so that if you come to the line feature and cannot see the control marker you will know which

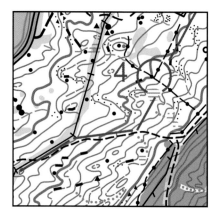

Cutting corners. Orange course control 4. The best way to find this control is to follow the path until it begins to bend, then cut the corner by judging the angle and aiming off to the wall above the control.

Aiming off. Orange course control 8. The distance from wall to wall on this leg is about 200m. Take a compass bearing to the left of the circle to aim off.

way to turn to locate it. Take a compass bearing to the edge of the circle rather than the centre of it.

Catching Features

At TD3 you could have a course with short sections without any line features to follow. Here you will be wise to take an accurate compass bearing and look out for a line feature behind the control which will stop you going too far if you miss the control. This is called a catching feature.

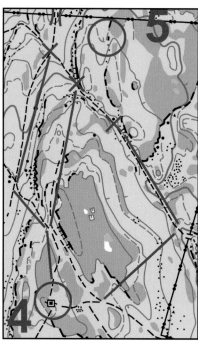

Catching features. The wall behind (north) the control is the catching feature. Whichever route you take, an attack point will help you to find the control in the re-entrant. The wall will 'catch' you if you miss it. Which attack point would you use?

Relocation

Relocation is finding your position when you are lost. Losing contact with the map usually happens because someone is running too fast and is a common enough occurrence. A strategy for relocation is therefore essential in order to minimize the time lost. At TD3 if you get lost, you need to find your way to a line feature junction or at least two very distinctive features in order to relocate. Stay calm and think clearly. If you are in a block of forest not on a line feature, which block are you probably in? Which general direction will lead you to a path or track? Take a compass bearing and go. Don't dilly-dally. When you reach the path or track, locate precisely on it before continuing.

The one thing to avoid when you are lost is doing the 'headless chicken' act. Once you start running round in circles, it is unlikely that you will establish your position and you will be wasting a lot of time. Following other people is also unwise. It will be just your bad luck that they don't know where they are either.

Look at the map that demonstrates catching features. Imagine you took the

Map feature	Write name	Feature name	Draw map feature
•—•—•—•—•		Fence	
(boulder symbol)		Boulder	
⌐ ¬ ⌐ ¬ (crag symbol)		Crag	
(footpath symbol)		Footpath	
••••••		Stream	
(powerline symbol)		Powerline	
▲		Fields	

A legend game. Fill in the gaps then check the answers with the legend in Chapter 2.

middle route and thought you had reached your attack point by the line of crags and boulders. However, you have actually veered eastwards and are looking at the next line of crags, which look similar. You head north-east looking for the re-entrant, but can't see it. To relocate quickly, head north to the wall and follow it west to the crossing point. If you see the control in the re-entrant on the way you are in luck.

For development of relocation skills, refer to Chapter 4 on advanced techniques.

Relocation practice task Take a map and go for a walk in an area with plenty of paths. Just walk without looking at the map, then after a few minutes stop at an obvious junction and see if you can locate yourself on the map. This might sound easy, but many orienteers find this sort of exercise quite challenging. Start with short distances and gradually make them longer between stops, also increasing the number of turning points. You are trying to remember where you have been, as well as setting the map and matching it with what you can see.

Safety bearings A safety bearing is a cardinal direction (north, south, east or west) that can be easily followed using a compass to lead the lost orienteer to a major road or boundary to relocate, or return to the finish area.

TD3 practice task Have a look at the legs on the 3 maps and decide which routes you would choose. When could you take a compass bearing or use pace counting? Which are the safe handrails? Would you choose an attack point? Can you cut any corners and aim off? Are there any catching features?

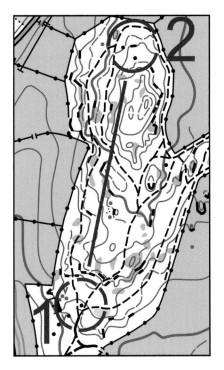
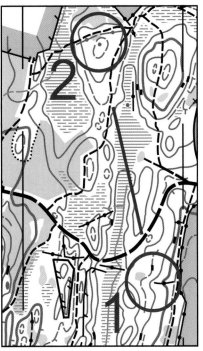
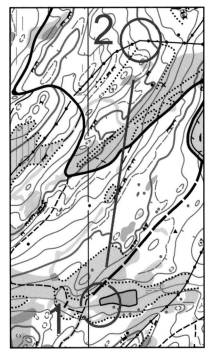

Route choice 1. Which route would you take? Remember to plan backwards.

Route choice 2. Which route would you take on this leg?

Route choice 3. Which route?

CHAPTER 4

ADVANCED TECHNIQUES

As soon as you have picked up the basics, it is time to move on to more technically demanding orienteering. These courses are TD4 and TD5.

The sprint course shown here illustrates the qualities of TD4. Many of the legs are very similar to TD5, requiring good map contact using contours, accurate compass and route choice decisions. However,

every control has a good catching feature, the attack points are all within 100m and the longest leg is 300m.

The planner has given plenty of changes of direction and a variety of control sites,

Light Green (TD4) Techniques

- Interpreting contour shapes on their own over short distances, or with additional information over longer distances.
- Taking and following compass bearings over longer distances against catching features.
- Using pacing for fine orienteering on short legs.

Green, Blue and Brown (TD5) Techniques

- Using contour shapes for most of or all of the leg.
- Using complex contours and generalizing contour detail.
- Undertaking courses that include long legs (1km+).
- Finding controls that are further away from attack points and catching features.

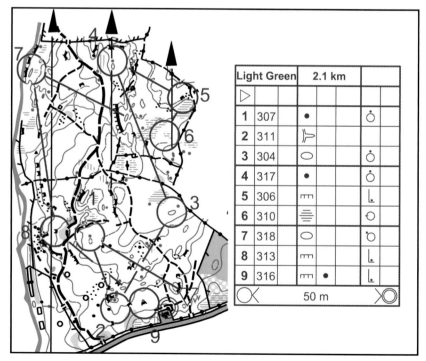

Light Green		2.1 km		
▷				
1	307	•		○̇
2	311	⏞		
3	304	⬭		○̇
4	317	•		○̇
5	306	⊓		⌐
6	310	≋		⊖
7	318	⬭		○̇
8	313	⊓		⌐
9	316	⊓	•	⌐
⊗		50 m		⊗

Advanced techniques are used to follow your route choices fast and fluently.

A Light Green (TD4) sprint course. Every control has a good catching feature and attack point. Notice that the red control circles and leg lines have been cut so as not to obscure useful navigation detail.

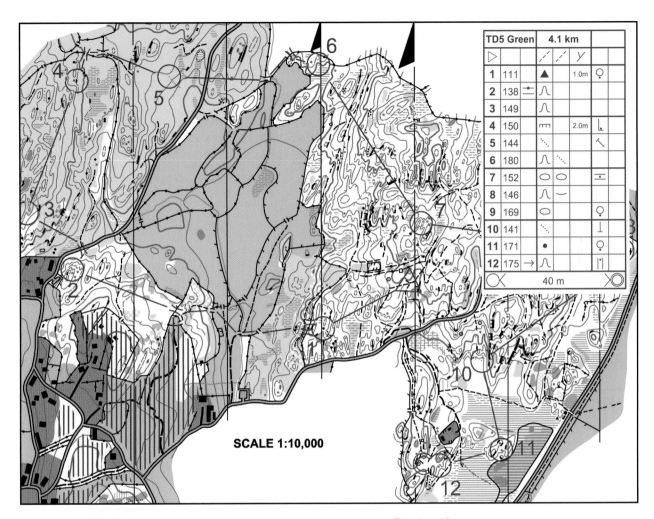

TD5 Green			4.1 km			
▷				/	/	Y
1	111		▲		1.0m	♀
2	138	⊢	⋀			
3	149		⋀			
4	150	⊓		2.0m		⌐
5	144		⦙			∠
6	180		⋀	⦙		
7	152		○	○		⊡
8	146		⋀	⌣		
9	169		○			♀
10	141		⦙			↓
11	171		●			♀
12	175	→	⋀			⎟⎟
⊗				40 m		⊚

SCALE 1:10,000

A Green course (TD5). All of the advanced techniques will be required to complete this course efficiently and fast.

ADVANCED TECHNIQUES TOOLBOX

Advanced techniques:

- reading the map
- map memory and terrain memory
- contour interpretation
- reading the map on the run
- effectively developing use of the compass
- distance estimation
- route choices
- selecting and using attack points
- route execution strategies
- relocation
- adapting to different terrain types.

which, as you should expect at this level, are on the far side of the control feature. The orienteer should find the feature, then look for the control referring to the control descriptions. Compare this course to the TD2 Yellow on the same area and the TD3 Orange in Chapter 3. At TD4 there is usually more than one route, fewer handrails and finding controls requires techniques found in the advanced techniques toolbox (see left).

The techniques and skills described at each level are linked with racing and completing a course efficiently and fast. You need to know what techniques you can use and then apply them at an event.

Most time is saved by choosing a good route and following it fluently, applying the right techniques at the right time. This is where the acquisition of these advanced techniques will help you.

Map Reading

Map reading is the basic skill of orienteers. You may be in awe of top competitors. How do they finish so much time ahead, even when you think you have had the perfect race? A top orienteer is running while continuously reading the map and reading the terrain. These skills are map memory and terrain memory; it is not just one then the other, they are simultaneous and that can be tricky!

A top orienteer is running continuously reading both the map and the terrain.

Map memory. Pick one control at a time, remember what is in the circle, then reproduce it from memory.

Map Memory

Map memory is the amount of information you are able to gather from the map in one glance. It is partly the ability to convert what you see on the map into a 3D mental picture and retain this information when other things are happening. It is also being able to select the important information and remember it. This is a skill that comes with practice.

Map memory practice task Do this inside, using the map on the left or any map with a course on it. Pick one control circle at a time, give yourself ten seconds to look at it and remember what is in the circle, then turn the map over and reproduce the control site, drawing it on a blank sheet of paper. Adjust the time to challenge your memory skills. If you are a person who normally sees pictures rather than words, you should find this relatively easy. If you are a word person, start with very easy control areas with minimal information and transfer with words rather than pictures. For example: 'I see a re-entrant with a crag above one side and a spur with a knoll on the other.' The 'picture people' will create a visual picture of the information. In your analysis, consider how much you can remember in one look and practise at your next event; only try to remember two or three features at once.

Terrain Memory

As well as reading the map and checking off map features seen in the terrain, experienced orienteers are also reversing this process by looking at the terrain and, whilst they are running, identifying distinctive features they see on the map.

One way to start doing this is when you spot a control kite not on your course. It must be on a feature on the map. Where is it on the map? It should be on your route, therefore you know where you are.

Terrain memory also comes in useful when you are trying to relocate and need to recall where you have been.

Interpretation of Contours

Map reading is about reading the landscape you are travelling through. Immediate and accurate interpretation of the contours and visualizing the ground from a quick glance at the map is the art of the skilful orienteer and one of the main skills to be acquired at TD4 and TD5. Every bend in a contour line will show a change of shape on the ground that will help you to navigate.

Contours at TD4

At TD4 you will come across sections of legs that require contour interpretation. A common situation would be from an

TD4. Using contours to find a control. You choose the wall junction as your attack point, then tell yourself and visualize before you move: 'I'll follow the right edge of the big hill (two contours) which the wall goes over, before I reach the end of the hill. I'll angle up the slope on my right looking out for the small spur with the re-entrant behind it.'

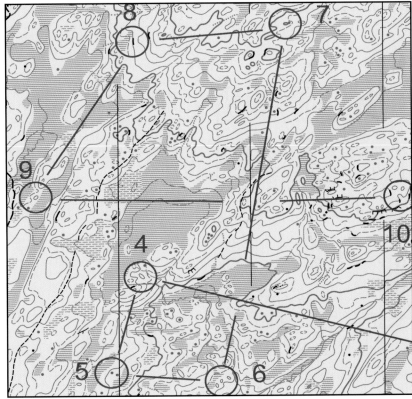

Part of a TD5 course. The planner's priority is to design legs that make demands on map reading.

TD4. Use the large contour features as handrails. The short tags show the downhill side of the contour lines and help on visualizing the terrain ahead.

attack point into a control, when you would need to combine careful map reading with a compass bearing.

Another example would be over a longer distance where there are other features to help you check progress. Follow the route from control 2 to 3 in the map above. Leave the path northwards just before it goes over the small spur. Follow the slope of the three contour hill on you right until you reach the next path. Look for the re-entrant straight ahead (north) which leads to the large flat area. Pick out the easiest running

line keeping close to the steep dune slope until the wide re-entrant with the stony ground. At the top of the re-entrant you should be able to look across to the cigar shaped hill in front of the knoll.

Contours at TD5

At TD5 a course planner will be trying to give you legs that make demands on map reading. The longer these sections are the better, because the best map reader should be the best orienteer.

When planning and following a route with only contours to help you, try to keep map contact by planning your route to deliberately visit distinctive contour features along your compass corridor. Visualize the landscape ahead so that you know where you are going. The course shown on the map can only be completed

Simplify the picture in the early part of the leg. This is a complex contour leg with attack points by the ruined wall. Control 7 is the knoll.

by good contour interpretation. Which major features would you use on the long leg from control 6 to control 7?

If faced with a complex contour section in the early part of a leg (see map on

The same leg with the early part simplified – just look for the major features.

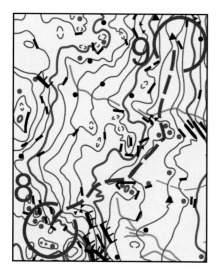

Contours can be used as handrails for route choice. The runner follows the re-entrant downhill until the ground flattens out. The flatter ground is shown by a larger gap between the contours; this terrace can then be followed to the boulder field and crag. The crags, knolls and stream can be used as check-off features.

previous page), it is helpful to try to simplify the picture by looking for the major features and landscape lines through the area.

In the example shown here you just need to go uphill about 200m to the ruined wall. The best route will be the one where you can keep your speed up. If you can ignore all the extra detail, the straight line option next to the steep re-entrant could be the fastest, but you might also consider following the line of marshes to the right. Both routes bring you to a good place to read the map carefully into the control.

If you find yourself having to map read through an area with complex contour detail the best strategy is to keep total map contact. As you progress along your route, try to visualize each small section and look out for the pattern of features in the terrain.

More Ways of Using Contour Interpretation to Improve Map Reading

Many contours can be used as handrails for route choice. A long re-entrant, a ridge, a change of gradient or a single contour line can be seen on the map and followed quickly and safely in the terrain.

The map-maker tries to ensure that the picture is clear for the orienteer running through the terrain. Features are plotted in an accurate relationship with other

A map with just the 5m contours drawn.

The map-maker has added form lines and knolls to give an improved picture for the orienteer running through the area.

Which of the twenty-two re-entrants are you in? Select a re-entrant and ask someone else to guess which one it is as you describe it to them.

DEVELOPING YOUR CONTOUR INTERPRETATION SKILLS

- Run with a contour-only map.
- Plan your route by checking off distinctive contour features.
- Practise looking ahead for the land shapes you want to pass.
- Visualize the main contour features along a route, then visualize the detailed picture coming into controls.
- Shadow an experienced orienteer who will talk you through routes.
- Take advantage of club coaching sessions.
- Do some mapping: trace every other contour off a small section of map then go out and fill in the gaps.

features in the area. Where the 5m contour interval misses detail and shapes that are clear in the terrain, broken contours or form lines are used to improve the picture.

It is the ability to pick up and observe these patterns of contour shapes that enables fast location and relocation. Look at this small area of map. Which re-entrant are you in? You should be able to locate by setting the map and observing the shape of the re-entrant and its relationship to the other features around it. Is it wide or narrow, long or shallow? Are there crags? Is there a marsh? Are there any hills or knolls on one or both sides?

A line that weaves its way across and around distinctive contour features.

Practice task Practise matching contour shapes on a map with the ground, plot a line which weaves its way across and around distinctive contour features, then follow this line slowly through the terrain. Visualize where the line is going, then look ahead and make the picture real. Do this for 50–100m at a time.

Reading the Map on the Run

An experienced orienteer will rarely stop to read their map. This isn't easy, but can be learned with practice. Start on a track or path system, then move into terrain.

An experienced orienteer will rarely stop to read their map.

First, always hold your map folded up and with your thumb close to where you are. Having a small area to focus on makes it much easier to pick up where you are whenever you glance at the map.

Next, look at the map in short glances, picking up more information with each glance. If you look for more than a couple of seconds you are likely to trip over something. Once you have picked out the area, look for the major features then look for the detail if you need it. You might have to walk to pick up intricate detail round a control. Make the most of tracks and uphill sections to make major decisions. Run with your map in front of you, not swinging backwards and forwards with your arms as if you are in a cross country race.

You should be able to take compass bearings and measure distance as you are running along. Try it when you go to your next event.

Practice task Go for a run with a map. Plan a route and follow it on the map without slowing down too much.

Choosing a Compass

Orienteers use protractor compasses and thumb compasses. When choosing your compass, it is worth trying a few different ones before you buy. If you decide on a thumb compass, select one with a housing that will dial. This means you can take an accurate bearing when you need it. Ask a local club member to look at and try a few compasses for you. If you can afford a compass with a fast settling and more stable needle, you will be saving micro-seconds and will run with more confidence, knowing that you are more likely to hit the point you are aiming for.

Using the Compass at TD4

Apart from the map, the compass is your main piece of equipment. Get into the habit of using it all the time to keep the map set, or to follow a bearing as described in the last chapter. At TD4 and 5 there will be many opportunities where

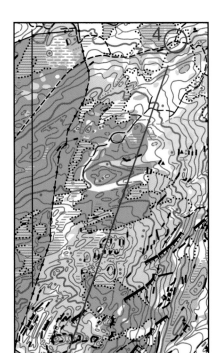

A long TD4 leg. Using the compass accurately will enable the chosen route to be followed confidently and without wasting time.

A thumb compass has the advantage of being on the map already.

using the compass accurately will be necessary to follow an optimum route without wasting time.

At TD4 there will be sections of legs where following a compass bearing will be the best strategy. The course planner will test compass with map-reading skills with a safe control or clear catching features behind control sites. These catching features allow the less experienced runner to minimize time loss through straight-forward relocation.

Using the Compass at TD5

At TD5 controls will be further away from attack points and catching features. More demands are made on accuracy of compass bearings, with time penalties for those who don't take enough care.

Compass on the Run

Protractor compass If you use a protractor compass, time can be saved by taking a bearing on the run. This is best done in stages so that you can keep your speed up.

Small errors in placing the compass on the map and taking the bearing can add up to a minimum of 5 degrees from the line you want to follow. Following an unsettled needle can add another 10 degrees to this variation. Always take a bearing as accurately as possible.

Thumb compass A thumb compass has the advantage of being on the map

---

USING THE COMPASS

Use your compass to:

- take a bearing
- keep the map set
- run in a rough direction following the needle
- find NSWE
- set the map to relocate
- measure distance.

TAKING A BEARING ON THE RUN

With each glance:

- find your place on the map
- place the compass along your planned route line
- hold firmly and check it is accurate
- dial north
- let the needle settle, needle north to dial north
- check the compass is flat
- look as far ahead as possible along the sighting line
- pick out a tree or feature to run to
- keep looking ahead.

already. If you can dial, use it to follow an accurate bearing, taking great care to look ahead along the line you want to take. If you have colour segments and no dial, keeping to an accurate line becomes more skilful and needs practice.

Fine Compass and Rough Compass

When using the compass, you should decide whether you need to follow it accurately, such as coming into a control – this is *precision* or *fine* compass. Alternatively, you may just use it to give you a general direction, such as running through blocks of terrain, aiming off or coming out of a control – this is *rough* compass. Always take a bearing accurately to minimize errors.

Running on the Needle

The term 'running on the needle' is used by orienteers who estimate the direction they want to go as an angle to the north/south compass needle. The following arrow on the compass gives you your line of travel as usual, but you run at an angle to the needle instead of dialling a bearing. Going north or south is straightforward; for west and east you run at right angles to the needle.

If you like running with your compass and map in the same hand, then running on the needle is basically a matter of keeping a sharp eye on the needle to keep it parallel with the north/south lines. Most thumb compasses are used on this principle. You are running, checking that the map is kept set with the compass. However, this is not an easy option, as watching the needle and map north can distract you from the direction you want to run in and everything else you need to do.

I prefer always to take a bearing, keep my compass in my non-map hand and glance from one to the other, either focusing on reading the map or glancing at my compass and where it is pointing to make sure that I am still on my bearing.

Using the Compass to Check Line Features and Slopes

When cutting through the terrain to hit a path, it is prudent to take a bearing along the path on the map and check that you are, in fact, running along the correct path.

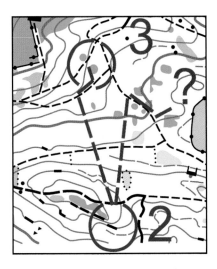

It is good practice to take a bearing along the path you think you are on. Here, the orienteer has aimed for a path and plans to turn left before the path junction to find the control on a thicket. However, he has run too roughly, hit the wrong path, doesn't check the direction of the path and loses time looking for the control in the wrong place.

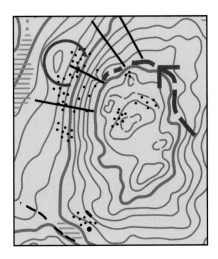

If you are running round a hill use your compass to check the angle of slope so that you know when to turn to find your control.

Running on the needle.

This doesn't take a moment and could save you a lot of time. Otherwise, you could well find that you have run down a wrong path the wrong way and finish somewhere you do not want to be! I find it quicker to take a bearing than spend time checking that the map is set, then working out why a path I am on doesn't match the way I want to go.

Another useful compass tip is that if you are running round a hill, knowing when to stop isn't always easy if there are no features to assist in keeping track of progress. You can use your compass to check the angle of slope, which will increase your confidence in making the next decision. I would take a bearing down the slope where I wanted to find the feature. When I thought I had gone far enough, I would hold the compass with the direction of travel arrow pointing down the slope; if the north needle was in line with the north on the housing, I would know I was in the right place.

Improving Distance Estimation

This section reinforces and develops the introduction to distance estimation in Chapter 3. There are many situations when relying on a 'feel' for how far you have gone will leave you hesitant and very often lost. One of the best skills to develop is the ability to look at a section of a leg and know how far it is.

Practice task Start with one scale of map. Collect a number of maps with courses marked on. Then, using the line scale as a guide, estimate the distance on different sections of each leg and write down your answers. Do a few, then check to see how accurate you were. Develop this practice with other scales and also mix them up.

Knowing how far you want to go is useful, whether you can just look at the map or whether you need to measure each section with your compass. You will need this skill if you are going to count paces.

Pace Counting

Knowing your pace count is a basic orienteering technique and can be applied in many different situations. It is preferable to get into the habit of counting paces so that it becomes second nature. Pacing accurately allows you to run faster without having to keep such close contact with the map in the early part of the leg. It is also invaluable when you want to find a control in featureless or low visibility terrain.

Always count double paces. Keep the distance under 300m if you want to be accurate. The chance of error increases the further you count. There are various ways of measuring distance.

1. Measure the distance using the correct scale on your compass, calculate the total paces then count as you run.
2. Alternatively, count in hundreds of metres, for example 250m at fifty double paces per 100m. Count fifty, fifty, then twenty-five. This way, you can adapt your count to the terrain, adding a few more if the ground is rough. Care must be taken to remember how much distance has been covered.
3. Another way of using pace counting is to count by distance off the map. Count paces to a distinct feature, then use this count to calculate other similar distances on the same leg.

Keep an open mind, try the three methods and select the one that works best for you. Do not give up just because it doesn't work the first time you test it out.

Using Pace Counting on a Course

You should have three figures you can recall for pace counting, depending on the terrain. Each of these is an average for 100m:

- a track or path running pace, for example forty double paces
- a terrain running pace, for example fifty double paces
- a universal walking pace, for example sixty double paces.

As you gain experience, you will learn to adapt these three figures to varying terrain and differing speeds. I like to add or take off a few paces from my basic count as the terrain or my speed varies.

Do not be over-optimistic with your estimated count. It's a miracle if you land precisely where you want to! Be prepared to be out by two or three double paces in each 100m. Remember it is a back-up technique to map reading and using the compass. If you think positively, you will appreciate the value of knowing when to slow down and look for the feature you want to find.

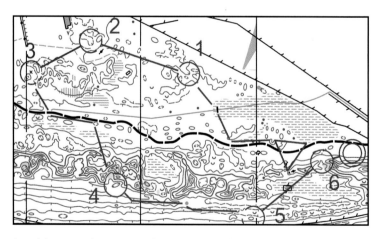

A sand dune area where pacing and accurate compass bearings help to keep close map contact. C1 – Pace from the bridge to the control. C2 – Pace all the way. C3 – Pace all the way. C4 – Pace along the track to turn off at the right place. C5 – Pace along to the small thicket, then again to the control.

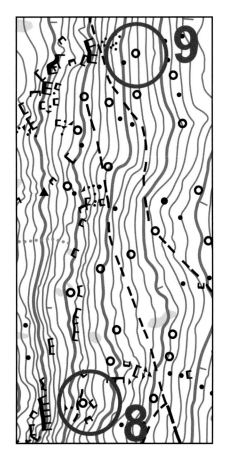

Pacing. A leg where pacing would help is the first part, in which you want to identify the indistinct paths as you cross the slope. What would you use for an attack point without gaining or losing extra height?

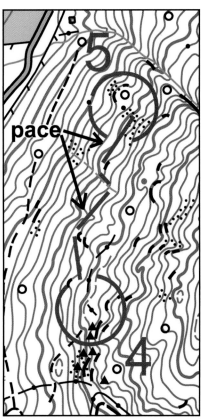

Pacing and aiming off. Pace and aim off along the slope to the ditch above the crag, your attack point, then pace and aim off above the control. You have greater visibility looking down.

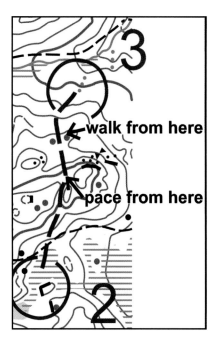

Pacing. A narrow marsh, which could easily be missed. Pace from the ridge, walking from the spur with the knolls.

Pacing and Rough Orienteering

Pace counting can be useful during the first part of each leg. In the rough orienteering phase, use it to help you check off major features as you cut through terrain and also to know when to turn off line features. If you are in an area with lots of paths, wildlife and competitors, you need to be constantly checking that you are on a mapped path and not on an animal path, or even an 'elephant track' created that day by runners. Counting paces as you cross through this sort of terrain is a great technique to pull out of your toolbox.

Pace Counting and Aiming Off

Using pace counting with aiming off can be useful when planning and executing a route. In the middle map above showing leg 4 to 5, aiming off is used in both parts of the leg.

Pacing and Fine Orienteering

Pacing is of greatest value in helping you to locate controls when it is combined with close map contact and a compass bearing. This is where a walking pace is invaluable to avoid over-shooting the control, especially in more featureless or low visibility terrain. Controls found by

luck rather than map reading are sometimes called 'bingo' controls. Finding 'bingo' controls in pits and small depressions in flat areas requires compass, pace counting and a sixth sense. Look out for competitors who have just found it.

Small depression. A 'bingo' control whichever way you approach it. A poor control site because there is so little map reading required.

The challenge is to make decisions as fast as possible.

Route Choice

A course planner will be trying to offer legs with a choice of route. Theoretically, these route options should be roughly equal. You have to spot the options and then decide which is the best for you. The challenge is to make these decisions as fast as possible.

If you have worked up through the colour courses and technical levels (and read the earlier chapters of this book), you will know about attack points, pacing and cutting corners using your compass. If you have launched straight into TD5, then you might need to check out the basic techniques so you develop good habits from the beginning.

Choose the route for the whole of each leg before you set out from each control, then stick to it. Planning your routes ahead of each leg is included in Chapter 6 on racing strategies.

Factors Affecting Route Choice

Straight or Round?

The classic route choice problem is whether to go straight or round. Is it faster to go straight but over the hill or across a valley, rather than the longer route round without the climb? A useful guide in making one of these route choice decisions is to look at how far away the contour, track or path is from the straight line at its widest point. This will be approximately the extra distance you will have to run if you go round. If you know you can run 20 per cent further on a road in the same time as going straight through the terrain, then you are beginning to accumulate information to help you choose your route.

Many orienteers like to go straight regardless of track options, choosing a route where they can check off features along a corridor, keeping an alert eye on the compass all the way. In the end, you will learn most from experience and talking to others and comparing routes and times.

Using paths and tracks give your legs and mind a rest from running through the terrain.

Using Track and Path Options

As well as using tracks because they are faster they also offer other attractions that should be considered when making your route choices. They give your legs and mind a rest from running through the terrain; they allow you to look at the next leg and even the rest of the course; using paths takes away some of the stress that can accumulate when concentrating hard on keeping map contact on straight line routes.

Finding the Controls

The major factor to be considered in choosing a route is finding the next control. Look at the area round the control circle on the map. Which is the best approach? Are there features near the control that will lead you into it? Will you need an attack point? With experience, you will be able to identify the warning signals from the map that indicate when you should choose an attack point.

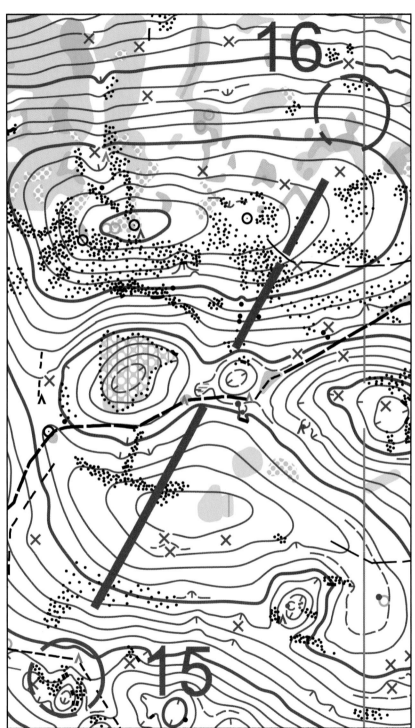

A world championship route choice leg. Straight or round? Consider the path options and how you want to find the control. A good leg for discussion as there is more than one answer. (Áron Less)

Finding the controls. Look for the features near each control circle that will make it larger and lead you into it. 1. Between the knolls: approach down the spur from above.

Make the control bigger. 2. Between the hills: use the large hill to lead you in from either side.

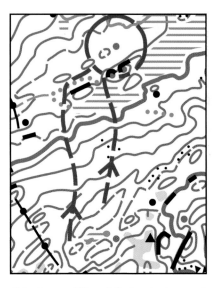

Make the control bigger. 3. Knoll: make the control 'larger' by using the line of hills and hills with the crags and marsh. Making a good mental picture of this control will help you to find it quickly.

Selecting Attack Points

You use an attack point to help you to find a control. Is it complex terrain with a lot of detail in the circle? Is the control isolated with few other features around it? Is the visibility reduced? These are factors that will help you to decide that you need an attack point. So you now seek out a large and distinctive feature that will be easily found as close to the control as possible.

Nearest is usually best, but other considerations should be taken into account. If the control is on a slope or in hilly terrain, approach from above as this will give you a better and broader view of where you are going. The best attack point might actually be beyond the control and could change your whole outlook on which route to take.

Line features will provide clear, safe attack points, but contour features such as hills or re-entrants with two or more contours are going to be big and provide you with a feature that is easy to find and give good access into a control. Imagine

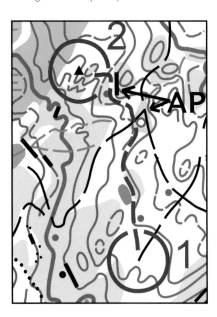

Use an attack point to help find the control. 1. Boulder field: in lower visibility using the ride junction with the large crag as an attack point should ensure finding the control first time.

that a one-contour hill of 5m is the height of two and a half tall men standing on

Attack point 2. Hill, north side. How are you going to find this control? What would be your attack point for this leg? Where will you start to slow down or focus more?

each other's shoulders. Can you miss it? Crags and cliffs shown with 'teeth' on the map also stand out in the terrain where two or more contour lines merge. Corners of vegetation changes such as

A long leg on open fell terrain. It will require a good route plan. Decide how you are going to find control 8, then plan the rest of the route.

thicker forest or large clearings can be used as attack points, although should only be relied on if there is a distinct vegetation boundary symbol.

Practice task How would you find control 8 in the leg shown here? Remember to work backwards from the control. Is there

A TD4 leg with plenty of scope for simplification. The only detail you need apart from the paths is round the control. This is the sort of leg where you have to think about orienteering fast and not just running fast. There is a risk of missing one of the path junctions.

a large or distinctive feature or features to lead you in? Then, look for any natural lines in the landscape that you can follow easily without gaining any more height than necessary. Can you see any collecting or check off features that will help you keep map contact as you progress? It's orienteering, so there isn't one answer: it's your choice.

Aiming Off and Using Collecting Features

Aiming off is a basic navigation technique. At TD4 and 5 it should be included in your route choice options to enable faster orienteering as well as leading you into an attack point or control. Wherever there is a line or distinct long feature that you want to pick up or 'collect' along your route, you can aim off to make sure that you do find and use it without losing time.

Route Simplification

As part of the route choice process it is useful to be able to pick out major features that you could check off as you progress along your route. This simplifies the route so that you don't have to keep such close map and terrain contact. Simplification will therefore help you go faster.

Identifying Navigational Difficulty

When you look at a leg and need to decide on the best route, try to choose a line which you will be able to follow easily. Is the straight line route possible? How much careful map reading is required? How much visibility is there? Try to choose the route that will be fastest for you.

ROUTE CHOICE

The following factors affect route choice:

- use of paths and tracks
- hills – how much climbing?
- terrain – easy or hard to run through?
- good attack points
- good checking-off features
- navigational difficulty of alternatives
- tiredness.

Look at this course. For each leg, ask yourself: How will I find the control? Is there a choice of routes? Is there one route that stands out? Leg 4 to 5 is the most complex because of the blocks of green (slow run). First, look at how you are going to find the control. I would use the ride junction to the south-west of the control as my attack point. Now you have the choice of keeping on a compass bearing in the hope that you can locate on the marsh and ride in front of the control, or make use of the marshes and keep map contact. I would go left of the line and pick up the track for some reassurance that I'm halfway there. Every time I cut through some forest I would try to have a clear visual picture of what I am expecting to see ahead – where I am going, rather than where I am.

Route Execution

Having planned your route, the real test comes in executing it – running and putting together all the techniques to find the controls as quickly and efficiently as possible. The more techniques you have in your advanced 'tool box' the more confident you will become at selecting the best ones whenever you need them.

The challenge of orienteering is to balance speed with certainty – running as fast as you can whilst knowing where you are. Your personal method of orienteering will depend on what gives you the most pleasure, satisfaction and success, as well as following your route efficiently. The tortoise and the hare analogy is illustrated at most events, whereby the slower but

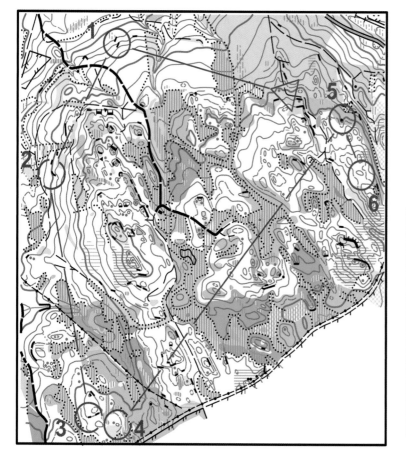

route choices				
▷				
1	31	↓	⊓⊓	∟.
2	32		⊓⊓	∟.
3	33	←	⊓⊓	∟.
4	34		◯	◯•
5	35	▲		○̇
6	36		◯	○̣

Look at each of the legs shown on this map. Try to choose lines that you will be able to follow easily. (Martin Bagness)

SUMMARY OF ROUTE EXECUTION

- Run as fast as possible to the control area, keeping map contact only as much as is necessary to locate in the area of the control.
- Plan the route for the next leg.
- Select an attack point or easily identified area within 150m of the control.
- Know the description and code number.
- Navigate into the control with the intention of finding it first time.
- Register at the control and move on as quickly as possible.

The challenge of orienteering is to balance speed with certainty.

more accurate orienteer will beat the faster runner who makes costly mistakes. There is nothing better for bringing a smile to your face than a competitor on the same course passing you two or three times!

Relocation

We have decided above that keeping continuous map contact just takes up too much time and running faster is the only way to get some good results. The penalty for this, of course, is the greater possibility of getting lost. Most people get lost close to the control they are heading for. The plan should be to reduce the relocation time to a minimum, for example the 20-min error reduced to 5min, the 5-min error to 1min, and the 1min error to less than 30sec. A relocation strategy now becomes necessary. The sooner you realize that things are going wrong, the better. It is much easier to locate when you know that you must be in a small area on the map rather than a large section where you will have to spend more time working out where you might be.

As soon as features stop turning up as you are expecting them to, there should be big warning signals telling you to slow down. Ask yourself when you last knew where you were. What have you done? What area are you in on the map?

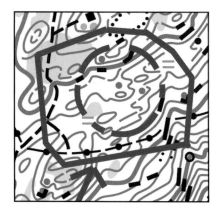

Relocation. It is easier to relocate if you can identify the area you are in by having a good terrain memory. You crossed the wall and seem to be between two hills but can't see the control. What might have you done?

Relocation. You crossed the ditch, are on a hillside but can't see the re-entrant. What might you have done?

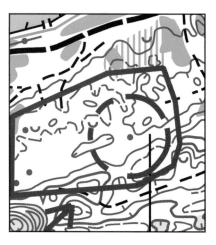

Relocation. You came over the dune ridge and can see small hills everywhere but no control. What might you have done?

You think you are near your control but can't see it, have you gone off your bearing? Did you take a bearing? Have you overshot or undershot? Can you see anything big that you should be able to identify? If possible, move up high to see more terrain. Keep moving for a short while to try to pick up a pattern of features that together you could identify on the map. Don't take on a 'headless chicken' performance! No luck? Stop again, think calmly. Set the map and look wider than the area in which you think you are. What can you see and can you find it on the map? Remember every place is completely unique. Also, don't dismiss the possibility of a 180-degree compass error. Could you have made a parallel error? Maybe you followed someone you thought was going to the same control – now, that's a good lesson to learn!

If you have spent up to a minute trying to locate and failed, the next step is to move as quickly as possible to a line feature you can't possibly miss. Try to make this decision quickly, take a compass bearing, get out to a line feature and then locate precisely on it before navigating yourself back to the control you missed. You will have lost time, but not as much as if you just ran around without a plan.

TIP

If you still can't find a control after you have located on a line feature, go out again and use a different line feature and attack point. The first one might not have been where you thought it was.

In the three relocation maps above, if you couldn't relocate in the control area where could you head out to and locate precisely? Now look at the leg 4 to 5 on the map in the route choice section (p.50). You decided to go straight on a bearing; you have crossed three marshes and have looked for the control for at least 2min. What would you do? It's possible that you are in a completely different block of forest. I would head to the edge of the open beyond the control then locate on the ride.

Mastery of all these techniques is the key to improving. In the racing and training chapters that follow you will be encouraged to analyse your races and identify skills and techniques that need practice. You may subsequently find it helpful to read about these techniques again so that you are clear about what you are trying to do.

PART 3

RACING

CHAPTER 5

TYPES OF ORIENTEERING RACES

There are many different types of event and these can be found on the British Orienteering website. Search for your nearest club and find out when they hold their local events, as these are the best for newcomers. Clubs hold orienteering events all over the country every weekend. They all attract the full range of age and ability. You can even spend your holidays orienteering abroad. Most orienteering countries have an event structure very similar to the UK. Orienteering maps have international specifications, so you could pick up a map in Australia or China and you would be able to read it as easily as one from your local club.

Racing Classes

In Britain at major events you pre-enter by age class. For age groups M/W18 and under there are A and B courses, where the B course will be shorter and easier. For senior age groups there will be Long (L) and Short (S) options, where the technical difficulty is the same but one is shorter than the other. These age group classes are the same all over the world.

Your Age	Your Age class
10 and under	M/W10
12 and under	M/W12
14 and under	M/W14
16 and under	M/W16
18 and under	M/W18
20 and under	M/W20
Any age/open	M/W21
35 and over	M/W35
40 and over	M/W40
45 and over	M/W45
50 and over	M/W50
55 and over	M/W55
60 and over	M/W60
65 and over	M/W65
70 and over	M/W70
75 and over	M/W75
80 and over	M/W80

Sprint races are usually held in urban areas.

Relay teams run in order.

At some events juniors can enter a class according to ability and not age. This allows juniors (twenty years and under) to compete on courses of progressive technical difficulty. So any junior orienteer can choose a course at a TD level according to their ability.

TYPES OF ORIENTEERING RACES

Sprint races – usually in urban built-up and park areas. The planner will offer route choice whenever possible. Winning times of 12–15min.

Middle distance races – these races are won in 30–35min.

Classic races – these are traditional races with a recommended winning time for each senior age group of 45–70min. Winning times for juniors are 25–40min.

Urban races – urban terrain with classic or sprint distances.

Team relays – teams are usually made up of three or four runners who run in order. There is a mass start for all first leg runners, which makes this form of orienteering really exciting. Courses are mixed up so that most runners out at the same time will visit a different sequence of controls. All teams run the same total distance. There are also multi-person relays with seven or more in a team, night relays and junior relays.

Multiday events – these take place throughout Europe during the summer and make a great focus for a family holiday. As in most events, everyone from young beginners to the elite are catered for. The most popular are in Scotland, Sweden, Switzerland and France.

Night events – any type of orienteering event can be held at night. A powerful head torch is a useful addition by which to read the map and see where you are going.

Score events – competitors have a limited time to find as many controls as possible in any order. Points are scored for each control found. Penalties are given for lateness.

String courses – young children can take part in string courses where they have there own simplified map and follow a line of string, finding control points marked by fun characters.

Read about strategies for these different types of races in Chapter 6.

Night events. A powerful head torch is a useful addition for map reading and seeing where you are going.

String courses are enjoyed by young children who have their own simplified map and follow a line of string, finding control points. (Robert Lines)

Orienteering is a popular activity in many schools and outdoor centres.

UK Junior Ability Classes

J – Junior M – Men W – Women

Classes	Distance (km)	TD	Colour
JM1 JW1	1.30–1.70	1	White
JM2 JW2	1.70–2.30	2	Yellow
JM3 JW3	2.20–3.00	3	Orange
JM4 JW4	2.60–4.00	4	Light Green
JM5S JW5S	3.20–4.80	5	Green
JM5M JW5M	4.40–6.60	5	Blue/Green
JM5L JW5L	6.00–9.00	5	Brown/Blue

Events for Schools and Juniors

Map reading is more and more being recognized as a life skill and orienteering has become a popular outdoor activity in many schools and outdoor centres. Orienteering clubs often become involved in developing local school leagues for younger juniors; these are school- or park-based and a foundation for TD1 White or TD2 Yellow races at open events. British Schools Championships are held annually for school year groups 5 to 13.

Racing is fun. You test your navigation skills against others and challenge yourself to find all the controls. Read on to find out ways to do this more successfully.

CHAPTER 6

RACING STRATEGIES

Experience is the name of the game. Sarah Rollins, many times British Champion, has run for Britain for more than ten years.

In the Race

You go to some orienteering events and you read the book to check up on techniques. This should help to improve your racing, so you then go to more events. Experience is the name of the game. There is certainly no one way to orienteer. The routes chosen and the way they are executed are all yours.

The advice which follows can be used at all levels, whether you are a junior or newcomer at TD1 White or an experienced orienteer at TD5.

RACING TIP

A short cut to improving your racing style is to ask someone to observe you, by following you round a course. This is called shadowing. You will be given advice and help to focus on appropriate race strategies and skills. You can also learn by shadowing the other person. Ask them to give a commentary as they go; this helps you to understand how to read the terrain and make appropriate decisions.

The Balance of Speed and Certainty

Racing is about running as fast as you can whilst staying in control and knowing where you are. To work your way up the performance ladder it is necessary to be fit enough to run hard throughout the length of a race.

The main doctrine to follow at every level is to think 'orienteering fast', not 'running fast'. Without the self-discipline of keeping your speed under control and maintaining some sort of map contact you will find you are putting in a lot of unnecessary distance.

If the navigation is relatively simple, you can run faster than when having to concentrate hard on keeping contact with the map. Using a path system gives you a chance to run faster, but make sure you keep your brain in gear. If you know you will have to run hard up a hill with the inevitability of getting into oxygen debt at the top, make important decisions beforehand. Be wary towards the end of a race when you are tired; adjust your running speed so that you stay in control. The successful orienteer is constantly trying to stay on the right edge of speed and certainty. It is all about staying in control.

Racing Strategies

The way you approach an event and decide how to race will usually depend on the type of terrain, as described in Chapter 10. Here we will describe some recognized approaches to route planning and route execution that can be used in any sort of terrain at all levels from TD1 to TD5.

First Controls

FIRST CONTROL STRATEGY
• Focus totally on what you have to do. • Find the triangle and control 1. • Make a prudent route choice. • Take a compass bearing if needed. • Check distance (know the scale). • Fold and thumb the map. • Check the terrain with the map. • Focus totally on the route execution. • If you are very nervous, just walk.

Racing is all about staying in control. British runner Rachael Elder; her favourite events are middle distance and relay.

control 1 - fodder rack

Control 1. Total focus is needed to find the first control.

After you have started off, one thing you don't want is to miss the first control. Losing time at the beginning can spoil the whole race, as it can be difficult to get back into a confident rhythm of racing. Timing starts before you pick up your map, so you are immediately under pressure to perform. Tell yourself that seconds spent now will save minutes wasted if you make mistakes. As you run to the start kite follow the first control strategy shown in the box.

Traffic Lights – A Route Execution Strategy

Green, amber, red. Fast, slower, slow. Rough, more careful, very careful. Wide focus increasing to narrow focus. Are you getting the picture? When you are deciding on a route, remember to plan backwards so that you select your attack point and approach into the control first.

This is your point to change from amber to red. In complex terrain you may have to slow down, but more importantly increase you focus. Your focus and concentration is directed totally on reading the map and finding the control.

Continuous Contact

Continuous contact is a good strategy to stop you getting lost and is advisable on complex terrain. You keep close track of where you are and where you are going. Keep your thumb on the map exactly where you are and look out for the next feature along your route. Those new to orienteering should continually match the map to the terrain in this way. As you gain experience simplification of your chosen

A traffic light strategy. Plan your route in three sections: green, amber, red.

Focus and concentration is directed totally on reading the map and finding the control.

CONTINUOUS CONTACT STRATEGY

Use a continuous contact strategy:

- when you first start orienteering
- when you move up a technical level
- in complex terrain
- when finding the first control
- if you are nervous
- if you lack confidence.

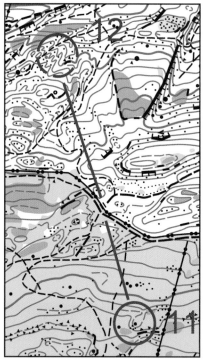

Complex terrain needs a continuous contact strategy. Which way would you go to keep contact?

route will help you keep in contact whilst maintaining pace, especially during the early 'green' part of each leg (see previous paragraph). A continuous contact strategy should be used if you are a bit nervous or lack confidence, as finding features you want to see is very reassuring.

Changes of Terrain Type

Different types of terrain make different demands on you as an orienteer. Race strategies will need to be adapted to the type of terrain within a race. For example, a course may go from open moorland into low visibility forest. You are running fast and keeping contact quite easily in the open ground, but as soon as you have to navigate through the lower visibility woodland you not only have to curb your speed but your mental approach has to sharpen up as you need to watch your compass more carefully and keep careful track of distance. It is where many mistakes will be made by the unwary.

On White, Yellow and Orange courses watch out for features that are not so familiar and be ready to focus more on reading the map with the terrain.

Change of terrain. This leg goes from open land into woodland. The orienteer should be prepared to curb speed and focus to find the control.

This orienteer is about to go into lower visibility woodland, so she will have to watch her compass more carefully and keep careful track of distance.

Race Strategies for Different types of Event

The different types of races are outlined in Chapter 5. All of these require a different approach if you are going to race them hard. Try to get into the mindset of the planner who is setting challenges according to rules and guidelines for each type of race.

Sprint races These require good speed, agility and power with total focus, as illustrated by the commentary by Pippa Whitehouse in Chapter 7. In urban races, controls will be easy to find, so a planner will set route choice problems with plenty of changes of direction to make demands on concentration while runners are moving faster than they would in rough terrain.

Middle distance races These are also relatively short and require the same focus and concentration as sprint races; map reading should be continually challenged and route choices demand quick decision-making, with good map contact to follow them through. Speed endurance and strength training will help you to keep your speed up, while map memory and visualization practice will contribute to more confident map contact.

Classic races To run well in the classic long races as an eighteen- to thirty-five-year-old you will need outstanding endurance fitness to survive 90min or more at championship events. Older age groups will expect to be out for 50–70min. Courses for younger orienteers will have a winning time of between 40–45min. Training should include

runs of up to twice this time to build up endurance fitness. On hot days hydration can be a big problem if you expect to be out for more than 60min. This needs to be dealt with by carrying isotonic drinks if you don't want to rely on the drinks stations along the course.

Relays Relay teams have specialist first, middle and last leg runners. The first leg runner needs plenty of 'cool' to handle a mass start and be able to think independently whilst taking advantage of packs of runners. Running with a pack is very exciting and fast, but mistakes can easily be made as very few will be going to all the same control sites. Middle leg skills include being able to run your own race and take advantage of others while not being distracted. Last leg runners have

Try to get into the mindset of the planner. Be ready for the type of race as well as the terrain.

to be ready for the possibility of 'head to head' racing with a sprint finish.

Night orienteering Some orienteers specialize in night navigation, running as fast as they would in daylight. Great confidence is required, as well as accurate compass and pacing skills. Training in orienteering terrain at night will build up confidence for all types of racing.

Score events With choosing your own combination of controls there is a need to see an efficient way to gain maximum points in the time available. The clever score orienteer will plan their route in loops of controls, always keeping track of time, continually reassessing and leaving a few controls near the finish that can be visited if there are a few minutes to spare.

RACE TIPS – ALL LEVELS

- Go slowly and carefully to the first control.
- Decide on a route and follow it. Don't change your mind.
- If you make a mistake, put it behind you and get on with the race.
- Keep focused totally on the race; don't let your mind drift.
- Always be planning one leg and control ahead.
- Be ready for warning signals, such as not seeing features you are expecting.
- On long legs, know exactly where you are when you come to the last line feature.
- Lost? Stay calm and think logically to relocate.
- Be prepared to carry liquid on long courses.

Planning Ahead and Control Flow

If you are enthusiastic to improve, one easy way to save time is not to stop at each control point. As you arrive at each control, you should already know the direction out of the control and the route you want to take to the next one. Registering your visit with an e-card can take no time at all.

Now, you can't do all this at the last minute as you need all your concentration and focus to read the map into the control. The best time to plan ahead is as early as possible in the previous leg. As soon as you have set off from a control, take the first opportunity to glance at the next leg. In a series of glances: look at the

Relay teams need specialist runners to be successful. First leg runners need plenty of cool to handle a mass start.

British athlete Oli Johnson shows that registering your visit with an e-card can take no time at all.

whole leg, select an attack point or how you are going to approach the control, and then choose the route. As you get closer to the control, check the control description and code number of the control you are about to find.

If you are racing on Yellow or Orange courses take advantage of any path or tracks in the early part of each leg. It is easier to read the map on a path so use these sections to plan ahead. At all standards, if you have a path or track section early on in a race, plan the next leg and then if you have more time look at the whole course and try to pick out any major route choice legs that will require extra consideration. It is also worth looking for any technically hard sections near the end that will need extra focus when you are tired.

To add to this fluency and rhythm you can introduce another technique into this process of control flow. If you want to set off from a control on a bearing, make the most of slowing down as you come into the control and, before you register, take the bearing along the route you want to take. You maximize the slowing-down period, which then allows you to accelerate out of each control.

Practice task Run a course that is a technical grade lower than usual and practise planning ahead as described above.

Use a path or track section for planning ahead.

Planning ahead. Plan ahead as early as possible in the previous leg. By the time you have left the path to find control 1, you know the route you will take to control 2. You leave control 1 and as soon as you are on the path you plan the route to control 3. Early on the path to control 3, you plan the route to control 4 and to the finish.

CHAPTER 7

IDENTIFYING ERRORS AND UNDERTAKING RACE ANALYSIS

To run a course where you don't make any mistakes is very unusual. Jamie Stevenson, a gold medallist and consistent World Class orienteer.

Common Errors

To run a course where you don't make any mistakes is like a dream come true. It is unusual, so don't beat yourself up if you overshoot a control, or lose some time on a daft route choice. The main difference between a good competitor and a novice is the time it takes to recognize that a mistake has been made, and then the time taken to correct it.

Coming into Controls too Fast and Not Being Careful Enough

Of time lost, 95 per cent occurs when approaching controls; even between an attack point and the control. Everything is fitting in perfectly, you know exactly where you are one minute, then suddenly the control doesn't appear where you expect it to be! Why? What did you do wrong? Were you going too fast to keep map contact? Were you too vague about an attack point, or just not concentrating on the map detail? Taking a chance or being distracted by other controls are both common causes of errors in the proximity of controls. Know the traps and tell yourself to orienteer properly. Slowing down coming into controls that are in complex terrain or low visibility should be top of your 'promise' list.

Practice Task 1 Practise relocation in the vicinity of control sites. Draw a large circle round each control site. In pairs, 'A' runs fast into larger area, gives map to 'B', who relocates, finds control site, then runs fast to next large area where the map is passed back to 'A' to relocate.

Practice Task 2 Another similar exercise is called 'Follow John'. This is done in pairs

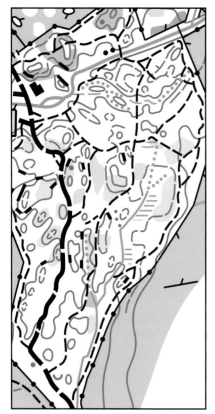

Careful placing of the compass on the map and meticulous dialling will give you confidence that you will run in the right direction.

'Follow John' exercise. Start off running round the paths and stopping at path junctions to pass the map over. Progress to cutting through from path to path before passing over the map.

with one map (no controls). 'A' runs through the area and stops somewhere distinctive, the map is handed to 'B', who locates, then takes the lead, chooses where to stop and hands over the map again. This is repeated for as long as you want.

Compass – Too Rough

The compass is an amazing instrument and, together with the map, gives you confidence that you are running in the right direction. However, you must always ensure accuracy. Careful placing on the map, meticulous dialling if you have a dial, checking the needle is settled, then following the direction in a straight line. It

is so easy to be sloppy and go off line by at least 5 degrees and even 180 degrees. Are you guilty?

Practice task To improve your ability to follow a bearing, practise running across blocks of terrain to very distinctive junctions following your compass bearing as fast as you can. Can you hit the junctions spot on? Do you have a left or right inclination? To keep on bearing, remember to look ahead as far as possible.

Not Finding Controls on Slopes

One of the main difficulties about finding a control down a slope is knowing how much height to lose. It is more difficult to pace accurately downhill or uphill, so there is an inclination not to go far enough because you don't want to lose or gain unnecessary height. Know exactly where you are at the top of the slope before you set off down. Use your compass to get the right line and if there are features you can pick up on the way, divert your route to go past them.

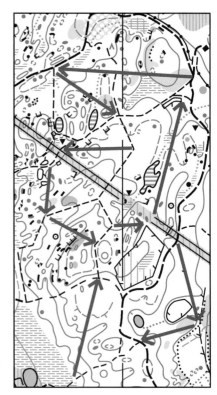

A compass bearing practice. Do you have a left or right inclination?

Slopes! Hill, north side. How would you find this first time? Know exactly where you are at the top of the slope before you set off down. What features can you pick up on the way?

Practice task Using an area with plenty of hills or slopes, take a map and run or walk up and down slopes with varying numbers of contours. The aim is to get the feel of what it is like to go down and up two contours or five contours, one contour or ten. First, get yourself a standard to work from, using the contours and features to register two or three contours of height. Then test it out; run up or down a hill for what you think is the right number of contours, stop and check the map to see how close you are. While you are doing this, look at the slope as well. What does three contours look like?

Parallel Errors

The map fits, but the control isn't there! Could you be somewhere else that looks pretty much the same? It can be easy to

Parallel errors. The control is on a crag foot on the right of a re-entrant. The map fits, but the orienteer has gone down one of four parallel re-entrants.

TIPS TO AVOID PARALLEL ERRORS

- Keep good map contact in complex terrain.
- Keep an eye on a wider route corridor to pick up parallel possibilities.
- Know where you are before heading down steep slopes.

---

think that you are following the features you want, but are actually following ones which are parallel.

Loss of Concentration

'I stopped to help someone then couldn't get my head back into the race.'; 'I saw a control I knew wasn't mine but just had to go and check the code.'; 'I was just so nervous I couldn't concentrate.'; 'As soon as I was overtaken I tried to keep up, then lost my concentration.' Identify typical situations where you tend to lose your concentration and next time you are about to fall into one of those traps, tell yourself in strong terms to focus on what you are doing. Using trigger words

Parallel errors. A hill by a marsh! Keep good map contact in complex terrain.

'As soon as I was overtaken I tried to keep up, then lost my concentration.'

TIPS TO IMPROVE CONCENTRATION

- The fitter you are, the easier it is to concentrate.
- Avoid too much anxiety.
- Learn how to relax.
- Have some trigger words to avoid distractions.
- Think about orienteering well, not trying to win.
- Smile – enjoy the race. Be in it!

such as 'concentrate', 'map' or 'focus' can help as well. Visualize yourself going through this procedure several times before an event.

To find our more about improving your concentration in a race, read through Chapter 14.

Correcting your Errors

Applying the right techniques at the right time and being able to navigate without making errors takes years of practice and experience. Every course you race is different, but you may find you are making the same sort of mistakes many times. The best way to start correcting these errors is to analyse your race after every event.

Race Analysis

While you are still at the event talk to people about your race, your route choices and consider where you lost most time. Draw in the route you took round the course and make notes against places where you think you gained and lost time. This is the time to identify errors and consider the techniques that require most practice.

Modern technology is very much part of orienteering. There is a variety of software that can be used for route analysis. You can put your route on a map with RouteGadget and compare it with others on the same course along with split times. You can also add your route provided by a GPS. This type of digital analysis can be included with recording your training into an electronic training diary (see Chapter 11 on physical fitness).

If you really want to improve, complete a race/event analysis form after every event. Provided here are two sheets that will help you assess your performances. Look at them before your next event, choose one, then fill it in after the event. In 'Detailed Race Analysis', tick the box linking the control number with the technique/strategy that went wrong. File with the event map and look out for correlations after a season of events.

Choose and copy one of the forms here. Check the Internet for results and note where you lost most time by comparing your split times with other competitor's on the same course. If RouteGadget is available, look at other routes and use this to help identify why you lost time. If you won, well done! Look at the fastest splits to see where others went faster than you did. Can you learn anything from this? Also look at legs where you have the fastest splits and recall what techniques you used. Can you remember how you felt and how confident or concentrated you were? Could you repeat this another time?

Keep a file of all your race maps and completed analyses and use it to plan some technique training. When you go to events that are not important, use each of these events as an opportunity to practise a technique that is causing mistakes or loss of time. At the end of the season use all your event analyses to make a summary of your strengths and weaknesses; this can be used to plan some technique training before the next set of races.

Two race analyses from two British elite competitors follow. Pick up on their mindset and their ability to analyse their mistakes.

Race analysis. While you are still at the event talk to people about your race and consider where you lost time.

ORIENTEERING EVENT ANALYSIS AND EVALUATION

Event ....   Date ....

Course ....   Length ....

My time .... Winner's time ....

Total time lost (est.) ....   Mins per km ....

1. Draw your route on the map

2. Strengths (what felt good today)

Leg	What went really well and why?	Est. time gained (check splits times with fastest)

3. What legs could have been improved

Leg	What do I need to do to improve this leg?	Est. time lost (check splits times with fastest splits)

4. Areas to improve for the next event (work-ons)

....

....

....

5. Other comments/notes, e.g. weather

....

....

....

DETAILED RACE ANALYSIS

Tick the box linking the control number with the technique/strategy that went wrong.

Event:	1	2	3	4	5	6	7	8	9	10	11	12	13	14	15
Ran too fast															
Too hesitant/slow															
Underrated difficulty															
Took a chance															
No attack point															
Poor route choice															
Did not follow plan															
Poor concentration															
Followed someone															
Distracted by others															
Distracted by other controls															
Didn't like the map															
Hard terrain															
Did not check control code															
Did not read description															
Tired															
Poor map reading															
Poor compass work															
Poor distance judgement															
Poor/slow relocation															
Stopped at control															

Graham Gristwood running for Britain. Graham is a multiple British Champion and was Relay Gold medallist at the World Championships in 2008.

A Classic Long Race Analysis

British team member Graham Gristwood reflects on his World Championship Long Race final in Hungary in 2009. Graham's ninth place was one of Britain's best ever performances at this discipline:

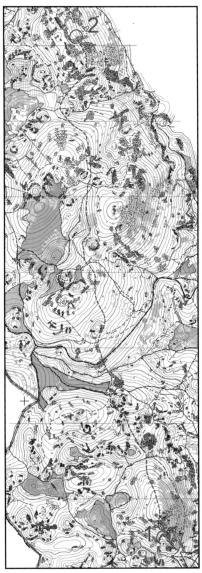

A World Championship long race final, 17.5km, thirty-three controls. The leg from 1 to 2 is over 3km. Graham's route is shown by the broken red line. (Áron Less)

			Long - final				
	MEN 1			17.5 km		750 m	
▷			╱╱			⊤	
1	31	↓	⌐⌐			2.0	♂
2	32		△	♧			♂
3	33		⌐⌐	⌐⌐	3.0 3.0		⊥
4	34		⌐⌐	⌐⌐	4.0 3.0		⊥
5	35		⬭				
6	36		⋀				⦙⦙
7	37		⌐⌐		5.0		⌞
8	38	→	⌐⌐			2.0	⚲
9	39		)(	▲▲			
10	40		⊩	▲▲			
11	41		⸪			○	☖
12	42		)(	▲▲			
13	46		⌐⌐		1.5		⌞
14	47		△	♧			⚲
15	48	↖	△	♧			○•
16	42		)(	▲▲			
17	43		⌐⌐		1.0		○ᴸ
18	44		⌐⌐		2.0		⌞
19	45		⌐⌐		1.0		⌞
20	42		)(	▲▲			
21	49	⦀	⌐⌐			2.0	⌞
22	50		△				
23	60		⌢⌢		1.5		⌞
24	70	→	⌐⌐			2.0	○ᴸ ☖
25	51	↙	⌐⌐			2.0	⌞
26	52		⊩	⌐			
27	80	↓	⋀				⦙⦙
○ — — —			100 m	— — —→			
28	90		△	♧			♂
29	53	⦀	⋀	▲▲			○
30	54	↙	⌐⌐		2.5		⚲
31	55		⋁	⌐	2X2		
32	120	⦀	⌐⌐			2.0	⌞
33	100		✕				⌵
○ — — —			140 m	— — —⟶○			

The long race control descriptions. (Áron Less)

I won my qualification heat, which not only gave me a really good start position in the final, it also gave me some belief in myself. I had prepared well in the karst terrain [limestone sink holes] and I was really excited about this race. The most interesting parts of the course were the route choice to the second leg, and the last loop in the steeper, greener area. We have done a lot of training in similar terrain, and often running close to the red line is quite good, as even on the slopes, the runnability is just so good. Therefore I chose the straightish route, maybe with a little extra climb, but no really steep climbs, and quite a nice attack point for the control. My execution was not perfect, a few times I could have taken better lines through the terrain, but I think it was a really good choice.

Controls 3 to 10 were interesting and fun, but most people didn't make very many mistakes here, the forest was so open and visible. I made a small mistake on the fifth control, when I lost concentration and direction while taking an energy gel, and ran round an extra hole, losing maybe 45sec.

The last loop was the toughest section, both because you had already been running for more than 80min, but also because 29 was running over a hill down onto a steep rocky slope, 30 was contouring round a really steep, really rocky slope for 800m, and then 31 was a really steep climb back over into a green area. Many people lost a lot of time and places in this last part, partly down to exhaustion. The high training volume I managed through the last year meant that although I felt terrible, I actually ran quite strongly, taking some places here. Ninth place exceeded my expectations.

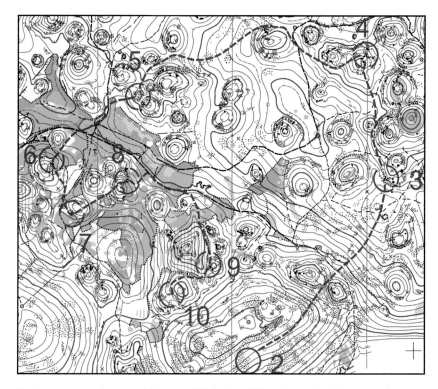

The long race course from control 2 to control 10. Look carefully and notice how this terrain is dominated by holes rather than hills. (Áron Less)

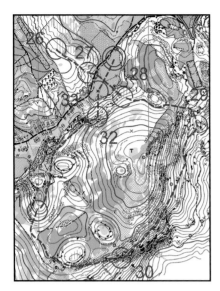

Controls 26 to the finish. This last loop starts with a marked route through the finish field to give spectators an opportunity to watch the athletes in action. Progress round the course will also be relayed to the finish with announcements given about best split times and potential leaders. This was the toughest section with more climbing and technical legs, such as 28 to 29. (Áron Less)

Graham took 1.43.49 for 17.5km with 750m of climbing – only 3min behind bronze medal position. The race was won in 1.36.31.

A Sprint Race Analysis

In this analysis, Pippa Whitehouse describes her thoughts and feelings before and during the sprint race at the same World Championships in Hungary. Follow her route on the maps as you read through the commentary and try to visualize yourself doing the running and thinking:

To understand some of the thoughts that went through my mind during the World Orienteering Championships sprint race you have to look back at my previous WOC races. I analyse each race in minute detail to determine where I lost time, what went wrong and why, as well as reiterating what went well. Several weeks prior to each World Championships I write down every

scenario that could prevent me from having a perfect race and either take proactive action (for example, pack a spare compass), or analyse how to deal with a situation if it arises.

The 2009 WOC sprint final was held in Miskolc Zoo and the surrounding forest. Before the race we had old maps, a plan of the arena layout, course length and the number of controls. As a team, we'd

Pippa Whitehouse in GB colours in a relay mass start. Pippa is a multiple British Orienteering Champion and has represented Britain on many occasions.

Sprint - Final			
WOMEN		2.6 km	105 m
▷		◇	
1	31	↗ ⌒	—
2	32	↓ ⌒	—
3	35	■	
4	36	→ ■ 4X4	·○
5	37	← ⌒	·<
6	38	← ⌒	Q
7	39	⌒	>·
8	40	↑ ⌒	♂
9	42	⁄	
10	46	⌒ —	
11	47	⌒ —	
12	48	V 4X2	
13	49	△ ♣	·○
14	50	⋔	Q
○——— 140 m ———→			
15	51	⌒	
16	53	‖‖ ⌒ —	
17	54	△ ♣	○̇
18	100	✕	
○——— 140 m ———◎			

A World Championship women's sprint race final, 2.6km. Map scale used was 1:4,000. First place 15.07min. (Áron Less)

planned our own courses and mentally run the race 100 times. I repeated my carefully structured warm-up from the qualifier, finishing with three 50m strides at full speed. I was feeling strong, and feeling ready; excited but calm.

Mantras

Heading into the call-up box I repeated a mantra of three words over and over in my head: Direction – Descriptions – Arena. I give myself a couple of simple tasks for the call-up and this steadies my nerves and gets me smoothly into the race. 'Direction' tells me to check my compass on the start line and mentally place myself in the map, knowing which way I'm facing. 'Descriptions' reminds me to check the control descriptions for any unusual features to watch out for and help my picture of the controls later in the race. It also helps me to understand the course layout, in this case a forest start, into the 'urban' features of the zoo, and back into the forest. I also noted many of the codes were in order, which makes them easier to check off. 'Arena' reminds me to check the layout of the arena. I quickly sussed out that the finish was on the same podium as the start.

Later, during the race, I used a different mantra, one which I'd been using all year, so it came easily whenever I was unsure of something: Plan – Precision – Picture. Have a plan for every leg, execute it with precision and have a picture of the control circle.

Start to Control 1

There's a short first leg and a route choice to 2. I set the compass for number 1 and run to the second surfaced track whilst checking the best approach to 2. I tend to make quick decisions on long legs because (i) you don't always have time to analyse them all in detail – pick one and check there are no dead ends; (ii) sprint route choices are often planned to be 50:50; and (iii) I'm rubbish at making decisions, so don't allow myself time to start deliberating! There's a good line to no. 2 from above; simple navigation to the crossing point at the zoo entrance and a handrail down the change in slope. Back

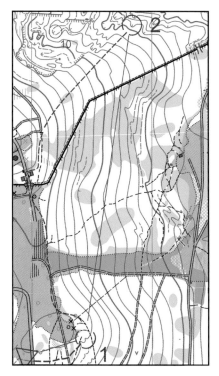

The Start to control 2. Notice the two crossing points. How would you know how far down the slope to go? It would be easy to make a parallel error by running into the wrong re-entrant. (Áron Less)

to the race: I cross the major track right of a bushier area and adjust my line to hit the first control cleanly.

Leg 1 to 2

Although I had decided to take the left route choice to no. 2, I was momentarily disoriented. My golden rule with sprint racing is always to know my direction out of a control, and I'd just broken it. I vowed not to do this again today and looked to my compass to get me out to the open.

Running to the zoo gave me a chance to look at the next section of the course. No. 2 looked like a tricky control, so I'd have to concentrate on the way in. I checked the route to no. 3 – no barriers to running straight, just push hard up the hill and then check my speed for the shorter legs. At the crossing point as I entered the zoo I started paying attention to the scale of the map and checked off the small buildings before cutting across to the dashed path and along to the junction. This was my attack point, and I knew I had to be hard on my compass from here. Looking to my left the gullies appeared, but I couldn't tell how far down I was. By my pacing I had a little further

to go, and was relieved to see the kite as I dropped into the blind re-entrant.

Leg 2 to 3

I knew my direction out of 2 and was straight onto my compass, picking the best line through the steeper terrain and attacking up the hill. I was aware of someone behind me – I'd been caught in a WOC sprint before, and had consequently rushed and made mistakes, but this had to be someone who'd missed number 2; they were going to be the one in a panic, so I made a mental note to allow for this and just run my own race: always know where I am going next.

Heading into the zoo, I clicked into 'urban' mode – navigating off very precise features, making it as simple as possible. I saw someone heading into number 9 on my left – useful to know. Looking up, I identified all the fences and buildings around me, and looked ahead to where the control should be. Everything looked right, so I checked my routes to 4 and 5 on the map and physically looked left along the route out of 3 as I was heading into it. A smooth punch at 3, handrail along the fence and look up towards number 4 to get a mental picture of where the control should be, again just out of view.

Leg 3 to 4

Once again. everything fitted and as I approached number 4 I could actually see the kite of number 5 through the fences, but I couldn't make out on the map whether there was a fence across the small gap between the enclosures – a potential short-cut.

Legs 4 to 9

Heading out of number 4, I looked along the gap and couldn't see a fence, so ran in. Bother. It's a mesh fence that you can see straight through and it's uncrossable. Putting the error out of my mind I executed plan B instead and sussed out the routes to 6 and 7.

The girl behind me had followed me into the dead end, so was now in front. I wanted a clear view ahead, so accelerated past her on the turn up to no. 6, but checked myself

Legs 2 to 4. Changing from woodland to 'urban' zoo. A different sort of focus is required. (Áron Less)

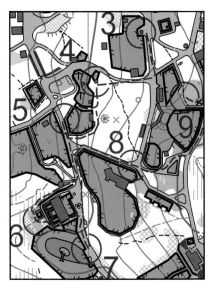

Controls 3 to 9 in the zoo. This might look easy, but decisions have to be made at top speed. Notice the mistake made between controls 4 and 5. (Áron Less)

not to rush. Once again, I knew which way I was heading out of 6 and ran smoothly through towards 7. Most of the legs in the zoo didn't require many decision points during the leg: as long as you kept your sense of direction and headed out of each control the right way you could pick up a fence and run along it, keeping it on your left/right as it bent round to bring you into the control. I knew my route to 9 from earlier, so picked the left route to 8 because (i) it was simple, just keep the fence on my right; (ii) it gave me a downhill run into the control; (iii) this way I'd see the control from a long way off so could plan ahead; and (iv) I could run straight through on my route to 9.

Planning ahead I still find it hard to plan a long way ahead in races and this was the first chance I'd had to look at the rest of the course. I knew we crossed back through the block of forest containing no. 2 as I'd been aware of someone running across as I'd approached 2. Number 10 looked tricky and I could see a safe approach into 11 from below. A quick check of my descriptions and the final few controls in the zoo went smoothly.

Leg 9 to 10

I'd decided to run straight to 10, but was careful to read all the detail past the central gully and made sure I was aware of how many contours I had to climb or descend. Where I reached the gully, there were several fallen trees on the far side, so I got pushed off my line and ran straight down the gully for 30m. I adjusted my bearing as I climbed out, aware that I should pretty much be at the same height as the control now. As I dropped over the earth wall, there was a girl sat in the forest to my right – a good sign; this must be the person guarding the control. At this point, it is tempting to lose focus and just keep running in the hope that the control appears. I checked myself, stopped for a second to read the map and remind myself of my control picture, then continued on my line and dropped cleanly into the re-entrant.

Leg 10 to 11

Once again, I already knew my route to the next control and gathered speed on the downhill as I aimed off to the right of the gap in the fence. I decided to drop quickly to the main track, which would mean losing a little height but would give better running and give me a chance to look ahead to the end of the course. I made a mental note that the next time I had to focus on no. 11 was when I reached the open area on my right.

Leg 9 to 10. Good distance judgement is required to turn off to the control at the right place whilst running downhill. (Áron Less)

Heading into 11 I mentally hesitated because the yellow area just before was covered with long grass, but I stuck to my plan and headed round the right-hand edge. The running was actually fine and I could focus on getting a good picture of the control circle. I was careful to identify the correct path out of the clearing, kept my line after the junction and dropped into the re-entrant just above the control. I was pleased I'd already decided on my direction out of this one as it was really bushy, but I knew if I just headed on down the re-entrant I'd pop out back on the main track.

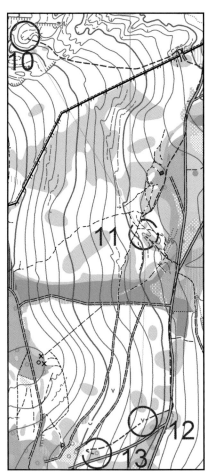

Controls 10 to 13. The road sections give opportunities to plan ahead. (Áron Less)

Planning ahead *Looking ahead to 12 the safest route seemed to be to drop immediately back to the main track after 11, but I noted that there was no good attack point to know when to leave the track again. Numbers 13 and 14 would require some hard work to drive on up the hill, then maximum focus on the spectator run-through. The last loop was quite short and didn't look too confusing, but I'd have another look on the run-through.*

Legs 11 to 13

I started to feel tired heading along the track to 12, so I allowed myself a mental 'three-second break'. Sometimes I notice my mind wandering and I start asking myself, 'Do I know the next control code? Do I know what's going to happen next — what is the next decision point?'

In such situations, when I'm running hard and am in danger of switching off, I make myself count to three; when those three seconds are up I have to tune back in — immediately taking a good look at the map and getting as much information out of it as possible now my head is clear.

I could see the track junction beyond 12, and was keeping an eye on the

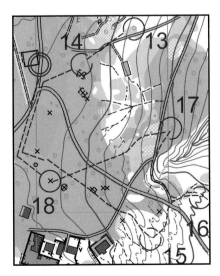

The last loop from control 13 to the finish. Control 14 is a spectator control with a marked route past the finish arena; potential to lose concentration. (Áron Less)

vegetation on my right. It cleared soon before the junction and I headed into the forest on a bearing, soon catching sight of the control flag. I knew I had to continue on the same bearing up the hill and that the next control was on the far side of a tree (so I wouldn't be able to see it). I sighted a large tree on my bearing, but neglected to check my distance and ran past my control which was in a bushy area. The semi-open area beyond the control acted as a catching feature — I was getting pretty close to it, so looked back and realized my error, just losing a couple of seconds.

Leg 14 to 15

Now it was time to run hard! The spectator control (14) was again on the far side of the feature, and it was 50:50 which side of the bush to run. I decided to go right to get a clear view of the run-through as I punched and because I punch with my left hand. From the arena layout we knew there was a bridge halfway along the run-through, so I worked hard up to this point, then had a good look at the last loop as the gradient changed to gently downhill. On my way past I also glanced at the last control (18), so I knew what I was aiming for on that last tough uphill leg. Looking back at the map I saw there were some black crosses that would guide me into 15. I looked up, identified them and accelerated towards the edge of the forest. I was finding it hard to identify the vegetation boundary heading into 15, but the black cross guided me into the right re-entrant and the control seemed to come very quickly.

Planning ahead *Glancing ahead on the map I decided to run straight to 16, but noted that I would have to be very sure on my compass on such a short leg — a small error in direction out of a control on a short leg means that you've run half the leg in the wrong direction before you realize, and this is tricky to correct precisely. Then I'd take the safe route left to 17, and straight again to 18 as I'd run through this area in the qualifier that morning.*

Leg 15 to 16

I wasn't ready with my bearing for the next leg; I headed out left, but was fighting to get a clear direction and didn't manage to pick a point to run to with confidence. I hit the track right on the junction before I'd settled myself and this came as quite a surprise as I'd been hoping to run straight through white forest. A moment to check the map and I had a new plan: keep right on the small track, through the clearing to the control. Because my picture of the control circle had been altered I didn't run this leg with as much confidence as I could have done, but it gave me an advantage for the next leg, as I would head the same way into and out of 16.

Leg 16 to 17

I punched, and was straight back up to the junction and running hard along the main track. As I entered the open area I tried to identify which tree had the control behind it.

Pippa Whitehouse: 'I had run the whole race with purpose, always knowing where I was going next.'

The one I thought it was had a large wire running round it – the radio to the commentary box, excellent! Once again, I ran to the right side to be able to punch faster and carry on running through the control.

Leg 17 to finish

As I punched the words of a spectator from my first WOC rang through my head: 'Now run as fast as you can!' I knew my direction out, I knew what I was heading for, and ran strongly up the hill, trying to keep relaxed so my legs wouldn't tie up on the run-in.

Along the run-in I could hear the commentator getting excited, but was aware he wasn't mentioning my name and suddenly remembered that one of the favourites had started 1min after me. I realized I'd managed to put this out of my mind for the whole race; I'd never been mentally 'looking over my shoulder', but had run the whole race with purpose, always knowing where I was going next. I was jolly well not going to be overtaken now, so changed my running style to a full sprint as I cruised down the far side of the bridge and, as always, pushed hard for the line. The analysing would come later, and I would find a few lost seconds here and there, but at that moment I was satisfied with my race, which is unusual for a perfectionist!

Pippa took 16.47min; 1.39min behind first place and less than 1min behind bronze medal position.

Pushing hard for the finish line. Matthew Crane knows that a race can be won or lost on the run-in.

IMPROVING RACE RESULTS

How to improve your race results:

- set some goals
- analyse races
- use RouteGadget
- use planning ahead and control flow
- improve fitness
- find a coach
- plan a training programme
- learn from others with experience.

CHAPTER 8

MOTIVATION AND RACE PREPARATION

How do you get a good result? Answer: by orienteering well. (Stephen Wright/BSOA)

Motivation

Goal Setting – Selecting Races to Race

If you are even the least bit competitive you will want to improve your performances. This can be done by analysing your races to find out which are your weaker skills, planning some training to improve your fitness and selecting some goals for motivation.

Select any sort of race where you want a good result. Just by doing this, your motivation and focus will step up a level. The whole prospect of having a result you will be proud of can be a bit nerve-racking, but a bit of anxiety and the resulting increase in adrenaline will help to give you the performance you are after. Tips on controlling anxiety will be found in Chapter 14.

GOAL SETTING – THE START

- Obtain a fixture list (BO website).
- Think about what results would make a good challenge and make you smile just at the thought.
- Decide on your goals.
- Mark the race dates in your diary.
- Make a plan.

Question: How do you get a good result?
Answer: By orienteering well.

Goal setting is not just about picking out a few races; it is also about being motivated by orienteering well. Select some orienteering goals that you will focus on during the races you want to do well in.

A good goal for someone doing a White or Yellow course is always to check the code numbers.

ORIENTEERING GOALS

TD I WHITE AND TD2 YELLOW

- Aim to complete three courses without getting lost.
- Use the compass to keep the map set all the time.
- Thumb and fold the map carefully.
- Run to every junction.
- Plan ahead – know which path to follow out of each control.
- Always check the code numbers.

TD3 ORANGE

- Decide on a route before setting off from each control.
- Plan each route backwards.
- Thumb and fold the map carefully.
- Only run when you know where you are going.
- Use the compass to keep the map set all the time.
- Take compass bearings to cut corners.
- Always check the code numbers.

The box contains a few ideas.

If you went orienteering every week and tried to race your best every time you would wear yourself out emotionally and find it difficult to concentrate at the level required to gain the results you are after. It is wise to select just a few races out of your annual programme on which to focus and prepare for in order to raise your results.

Race Preparation

To race successfully you need to sign up to the 'four Cs': Commitment, Confidence, Control and Concentration. To feel confident you must have self-belief, that is, believe that you have the skills and ability to achieve the goals to which you aspire. You can build confidence by committing to your goals and good preparation. Confidence also leads to a relaxed mind, which enables good concentration and control. The amount of preparation you decide to do will depend on your interest and level of commitment. Dip into the lists in the boxes and see how this affects your results.

RACE PREPARATION – ONE YEAR OR MORE AHEAD

- Plan your race programme.
- Select the races that matter most.
- Plan your training programme.
- Design your warm-up routine.
- Write it all down.

RACE PREPARATION – ONE MONTH OR MORE AHEAD

- Look at maps of the area or similar areas.
- What strategies will be needed to be accurate?
- Train on the same terrain type.
- Train at the same time of day as your run.
- Check your social diary to ensure adequate sleep.

To race successfully you need to sign up to the 'four Cs'.

On race day arrive in plenty of time. Can you see the last control?

On the start line. Remind yourself that you are there to enjoy the day.

RACE PREPARATION – ONE OR TWO WEEKS AHEAD

- Plan travel and race day routine.
- How far is the start?
- When will you start warming up?
- Read all you can about the event.
- What is the map scale?
- Have you got the right scale on your compass?
- Have you got a control description holder to put on your wrist?
- Have you got an old map of the area to look at?
- What sort of terrain is it?
- Visualize yourself orienteering well.

RACE PREPARATION – ON THE DAY

- Arrive in plenty of time.
- Stick to your race day routine.
- Warm up properly.
- Check the start and finish systems.
- Can you see the last control?
- Wrap tape round your shoe laces to ensure they don't come undone.
- Allow yourself extra time to catch up with friends you may only see at events.

START

- Get to the start with at least 10min to spare.
- If you have a start time, check the clock when you arrive at the event.
- Watch how the system works.
- Finish your warm-up routine with dynamic stretches and lift your heart rate with short sprints.
- Focus on how you are going to approach the race.
- Relax to avoid or reduce anxiety – keep active or chat to friends.
- Remind yourself you are there to enjoy the day!
- When you get the map, check it is the right course and locate on the triangle.
- Go very carefully to the first control.

CHAPTER 9

WARMING UP

The warm-up is a key part of preparing for any race or training session. It prepares cardiorespiratory and musculoskeletal systems to meet the demands of the exercise ahead. Undertaking a well-planned warm-up also contributes to bringing your mind into focus, overall confidence and a positive attitude towards the forthcoming race or training session.

It is recommended that dynamic exercises as described below are included in a warm-up. Current thinking is to use traditional static stretches as a separate session in-between training sessions or races.

Time/distance	Movement
30sec	Move head/neck gently to left, middle; right, middle; forward, middle; back, middle
30sec	Arm/shoulder rotations
2 × 20m	High knees
2 × 20m	Lunge walk
2 × 20m	Heel flicks (not bringing heel to kick bottom, but bring heel up to the bottom, then through quickly)
2 × 20m	Carioca – moving to the right, the left leg goes alternately behind then in front as the whole body moves to the right (face the same direction out and back)
4 × 60m accelerations	Go from standing to fast over the first 30m, then maintain that pace for the next 30m; keep the running style fluid and comfortable, don't strain

The carioca step; the warm-up is a key part of preparing for any race or training session.

Warm-Up: Example 1

Spend 5–10min starting with jogging, then increase the pace to a steady run. You should be slightly out of breath and beginning to sweat. The heart rate is elevated without fatigue. Follow this with some dynamic stretching exercises as shown in the chart on the previous page.

Exercise	Description
Walking on the balls of the feet	Walk on the balls of the feet by maintaining correct arm mechanics and an upright position
Can-can	Perform a running march with a high extended step
Small skip	Using a small skip, work off the ball of the foot, raising the knee to about a 45–55-degree angle whilst moving forward
Claw backs	As above, but bring the foot down to scrape the floor
Heel kick	Kick the heels towards the buttocks, raising the knee to about a 45–55 degree angle whilst moving forward
Single knee dead-leg lift (right)	Bring the right knee quickly up to a 90-degree angle whilst moving forward; the left knee should remain as straight as possible with a very short lift away from the ground throughout the movement
Single knee dead-leg lift (left)	Change over right/left
High knee run	Raise the right knee, then the left knee to about a 90-degree angle whilst moving forward

High knees. One of the dynamic stretching exercises.

Warm-Up: Example 2

This warm-up (above) is condensed to eight dynamic stretching exercises. They are designed to mimic running movements and progress from moderate to high intensity. Each exercise should cover 15m; follow this by 15m walk and then 15m exercise again. Repeat this sequence twice for each exercise. It will take about 9min.

Aim to maintain proper form and technique with short ground contact time. If you are unsure how to perform these, it is best to consult a fitness coach.

Race Warm-Ups

Many events have long walks to the start. You can incorporate these into your warm-up. When you are about a 5–10-minute jog away from the start, commence your warm-up and finish it close to the start area. If the way to the start is very steep, it may be that simply walking up will do instead of the jogging, then when you are near to the start complete the rest of the warm-up.

Mental Warm-Ups

When warming up for a race you should begin to focus your mind on the task ahead. Suggestions for mental warm-ups are given in the box. Aim to finish your warm-up just a couple of minutes before your start time. When you finish the mental warm-up and approach the start you should be completely focused on orienteering.

An alternative is to do your race thinking at home and just relax during the warm-up and only 'switch on' just before the start. Experiment at less important events. Try different mental warm-ups until you find one you like, then stick to it.

MENTAL WARM-UP THOUGHTS

- Begin to think about your race plan.
- Look around at the terrain and think about the type of area you are about to run in.
- Consider the style of orienteering that is most appropriate for you in this sort of terrain.
- Plan how you will approach the first few controls.

CHAPTER 10

RACING IN BRITAIN AND ABROAD

Adapting to Different Terrain Types

As you race in more and more events you will learn to adapt to different types of terrain and to adjust your route planning and execution strategies to the area you are competing in. Many event areas will have a combination of terrain types and you will have to adapt your style as you pass from one to another. Course planners will often deliberately take you from a fast runnable section into lower visibility to test your ability to change from one strategy to another under race conditions. Before you go to an event, refer to the terrain type described below to check that you are familiar with the best race strategies and techniques to use.

TYPES OF ORIENTEERING TERRAIN IN THE UK

There are various types of orienteering terrain in the UK:

- open mature woodland
- areas with complex contour detail
- low-visibility woodland
- open or wooded sand dunes
- open fell, moorland, parkland
- urban areas – streets and parkland
- rough areas of heather, tussocks, marsh and so on.

Open Mature Woodland

For most athletes this is the most pleasant orienteering, when you can run easily, see where you are and where you are going. It is orienteering which requires map and compass skills that go alongside wise route

Orienteers gather at multi-day events, which take place all over the world.

choice decisions and good control flow. Good concentration is important as mistakes will be costly, with the chance of some competitors having a 'perfect' race.

There is a wide range of complexity within this category, from very open public areas with path networks common in the south of England, to remote pathless areas with plenty of complex contour detail found in the far north.

Areas with Complex Contours

A planner will be delighted to plan courses in areas where there is plenty of contour detail, because testing an orienteer's map-reading ability is always top of the list of challenges to be offered. The problems to be tackled include: finding controls on slopes where losing or gaining unnecessary height costs a lot of time; finding controls as far from a good attack point as can be found; and finding controls on one of multiple similar features. You, the orienteer, will need to slow down considerably in these areas and read the map feature to feature if you are going to find your controls first time. Always know how you are going to approach each control. Select a good attack point if needed and try to make the controls 'larger', as described in Chapter 4. You should be pleased to find controls by reading the map carefully, walking in from your attack point and without hesitation.

Mature woodland requires confident map reading on straight line routes.

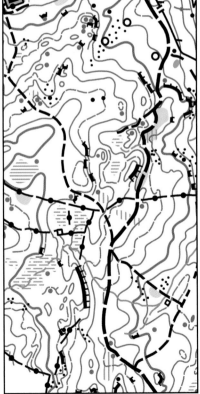

All white; an area of mature woodland in northern England.

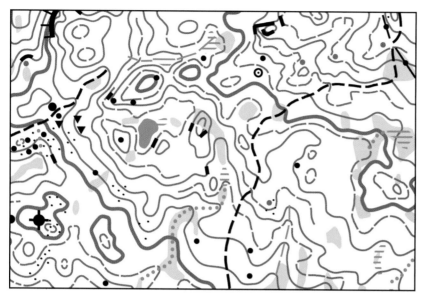

Woodland with complex contours. These areas present challenging and enjoyable orienteering. They require good map contact, especially near controls.

Low-visibility terrain. The two shades of green show different grades of runnability and visibility. The dotted vegetation boundary symbols show the clear divisions between two types of woodland. Low-visibility terrain requires a determined, positive attitude combined with accurate compass use and pacing.

Low-Visibility Woodland

Low-visibility woodland consists of areas where the trees are planted close together, or are very young and bushy. Reduced visibility means that you are forced to slow down, but you need a lot of concentration to maintain map contact through accurate compass work and good distance judgement.

Planning your route to 'collect' features will help you to keep contact. It is best to plan where you are going and what features you want to reach, more than trying to keep close map contact with features you can't see clearly in the terrain. This is where using a thumb compass and running on the needle may let you down, so keep checking your direction. Determination and concentration are also needed to run aggressively through this sort of terrain. If you let it slow you down too much, you will lose sense of the distance covered as well as finding that your mind drifts. Relocation is difficult in low visibility, so don't waste time if you get lost; get out and locate on a line feature.

Open or Wooded Sand Dunes

The coastline of Britain provides areas of sand dunes, which offer a special type of orienteering. They are characterized by huge depressions as well as dunes with steep sides. There will be sections with multiple bumps and dips, all very carefully mapped as knolls and depressions and providing the potential for control sites.

These maps have a contour interval of 2.5m instead of the usual 5m and if very complex will be at a larger scale than normal. There is scope for parallel errors, so good map contact is essential. To maximize speed it is important to identify good check-off features, with power running between. Approaching controls needs total focus, with visualization of the relationship of features in the circle. This is especially so in wooded dune terrain where the visibility can be greatly reduced.

Open areas require good fitness, as well as confidence within the control circle.

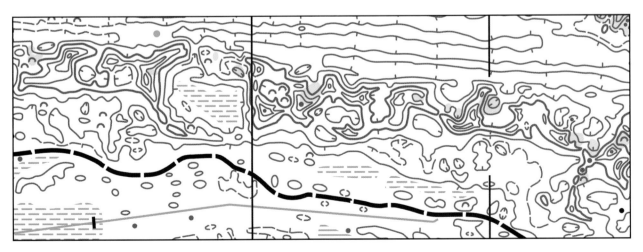

A sand dune area. The maps have a contour interval of 2.5m and will usually be a larger scale than normal. Good map contact is essential, using check-off features to maximize speed.

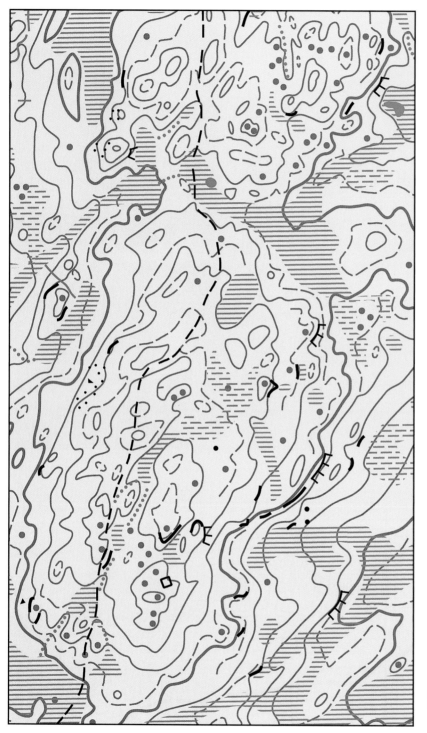

Northern England, Scotland and Ireland have many areas of moorland that provide interesting orienteering.

Open Terrain: Parkland, Moorland, Fell

Open terrain makes orienteering relatively easy because you can see so much further than you can in woodland. If there is plenty of detail, you should be able to run confidently while keeping rough map contact. However, it is surprisingly easy to miss controls, so always know how you are going to attack each control and be prepared to slow down as you get close to the circle. On flatter and more featureless areas, it is worth keeping a pace count to check your distance and follow your compass accurately, picking out features to aim for as far ahead as possible.

Urban Areas: Streets, Parkland

Urban street races have become popular in the UK and internationally. These are

Urban and parkland areas require high speed and concentration to make quick route choice decisions.

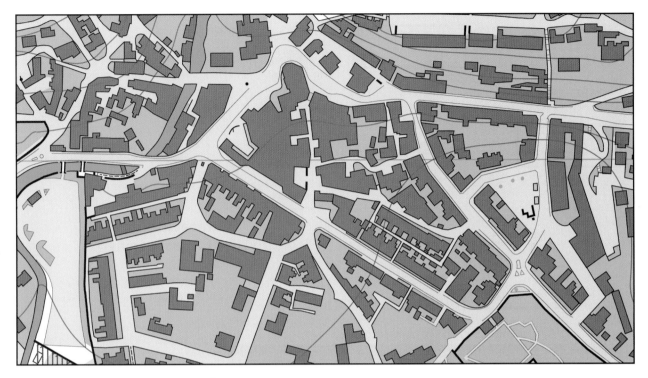

Urban maps are now drawn to international specifications.

Rough terrain requires an aggressive, determined approach.

usually 'sprint races', and require endurance and 'sprinting' decision-making. The technical difficulties in these types of terrain are not so much about complex map reading, as making quick decisions about routes and keeping very close contact with the map whilst planning ahead and running as fast as possible. There will be seconds between the top runners, so any hesitations or mistakes will be costly. Read Pippa Whitehouse's course commentary from a World Championship sprint race in Chapter 7.

Rough Heather, Tussocks, Felled, Marshy Ground and Slow Run

In any area where the terrain is rough and difficult to run through, fitness becomes a priority if you want success. You need to focus your training in the same type of terrain, working on strength and endurance. Your running style should be adapted so that you can lift your knees to run over this rough ground, rather than allow yourself to be swallowed up by it. All these areas, but especially rough woodland with lots of understorey, will need an aggressive, determined approach; this helps to give you a positive attitude, which should then help to dismiss negative thoughts towards the race. Good mobility and flexibility are essential for fluid negotiation of the 'ruf stuff'.

Racing for Britain

British Orienteering has a very clear Elite Athlete Development Pathway. This sets out a process for athletes, coaches, parents and clubs to refer to. It shows the progressions from basic junior and senior club level orienteering to talent identification squads and training at regional then national level. Selections for squads and teams are made based on race results. At each level there is a support network of coaches who direct

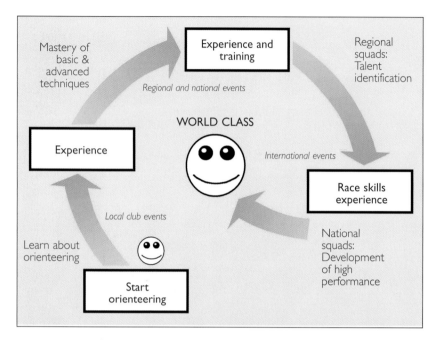

Mastery of basic & advanced techniques

Experience and training

Regional and national events

Regional squads: Talent identification

WORLD CLASS

Experience

International events

Learn about orienteering

Local club events

Race skills experience

Start orienteering

National squads: Development of high performance

The Elite Athlete Development Pathway.

or advise on training and race preparation. Any athlete can use it to identify where they are on the grid and to assess areas for improvement. It takes about seven years for a senior orienteer to become world class and twelve years for a junior. Details about selection for squad and teams can be found on the British Orienteering website.

International Orienteering

To run in a national team at the Senior or Junior World Championships is an achievement worth aspiring to. However, there are many other opportunities to race abroad. Orienteers gather at multiday events, which take place all over the world. All of these events will have classes for all ages and abilities. They are very sociable and provide a chance to analyse your races and try to improve each day.

If you are over thirty-five, there is an open Masters or Veteran World Championship, which takes place in a different country each year. At this event there are classes and medals to be won for thirty-five- to ninety-year olds. There isn't any selection and no minimum standard, although qualification races will divide each class into A and B finals.

Jamie Stevenson racing for Britain.

PART 4
TRAINING

CHAPTER 11

PHYSICAL FITNESS

Of course, fitness plays a huge part in orienteering success. Another great advantage of being fitter is that running requires less mental effort, so that you can apply your concentration to finding controls. On average, if an experienced orienteer takes 50min to complete a course, 45min (80 per cent) is running and 5min (10 per cent) is reading the map and finding controls. If you try to run flat out, you get into oxygen debt and can't make sensible decisions, so you orienteer at around 80 per cent of your maximum long-distance speed to enable you to concentrate.

General Fitness

Orienteering involves running across country with short pauses and extra efforts, usually taking between 40min and 90min. It requires endurance, speed, strength and mobility. Fitness training is about making the body exercise more efficiently. The body works best when it is fuelled with the right diet and an efficient oxygen transport system. Oxygen has a critical role to play in the production of energy. As your heart rate increases, you automatically breathe more rapidly to take in and absorb more oxygen. By deliberately increasing the heart rate and working the muscles harder than usual, the body will adapt to this challenge and a more efficient system results. The classic advice is that you should be 'puffing'; you must increase your heart rate if you want to be fitter. This is aerobic exercise and develops your aerobic capacity.

During aerobic exercise the body works steadily, making demands on oxygen consumption without going into oxygen debt. Aerobic exercise would include circuit training, swimming, cycling,

hill walking, sports which include running, such as football, rugby and hockey as well as cross-country and fell running. Whatever you choose to do, try to exercise a minimum of three or four times a week.

Anaerobic exercise is much harder, because you are deliberately working in a

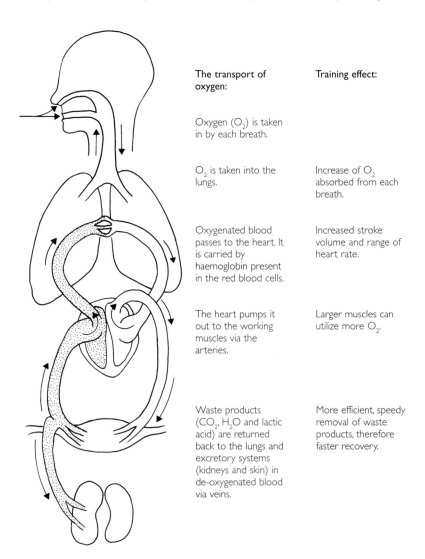

The transport of oxygen:	Training effect:
Oxygen (O_2) is taken in by each breath.	
O_2 is taken into the lungs.	Increase of O_2 absorbed from each breath.
Oxygenated blood passes to the heart. It is carried by haemoglobin present in the red blood cells.	Increased stroke volume and range of heart rate.
The heart pumps it out to the working muscles via the arteries.	Larger muscles can utilize more O_2.
Waste products (CO_2, H_2O and lactic acid) are returned back to the lungs and excretory systems (kidneys and skin) in de-oxygenated blood via veins.	More efficient, speedy removal of waste products, therefore faster recovery.

A simplified diagram of the oxygen transport system.

state of oxygen debt. This can be included in training programmes after a good basic fitness has been achieved. Check out some websites for more detail.

Running Training Stage 1

Orienteering is a running sport, so this is the best place to start. It's simple: you want to be able to run continuously for the length of time you are usually out on an orienteering course, therefore that is your first goal. Plan to go out for three aerobic runs a week; start with 10min, then gradually add another 5 or 10min until you have reached your goal. If it is dark when

---

RUNNING TRAINING

- Keep off the roads as much as possible.
- Go out with friends or a running group.
- Talking while you run keeps the pace steady.
- Start steadily and aim to keep going without stopping.
- Plan a variety of routes.
- Take an 'O' map with you and practise reading it on the run.
- Don't run if you feel unwell.
- Don't hang around in damp, sweaty clothes.
- Check your diet, especially for iron and vitamin C; these are needed to transport oxygen.

---

you have time to train, it is worth including a gym or fitness circuit once a week. The one shown on the next page could be set up at home if you haven't access to a gym. You will start feeling the positive effects of training after a few weeks. Your race results will improve straight away as long as you don't speed off without looking at the map. Before you do any more training, check that you are warming up well before each run and consider joining a running group which includes running drills; these make your running style more efficient.

Circuit Training

A circuit is a mix of eight to ten exercises designed to improve general or specific

Orienteering is a running sport. Once you start training your results will start to improve straight away.

fitness. They can be made to satisfy most strength, speed and endurance demands. They are particularly good for working on flexibility and core stability, as well as general aerobic fitness.

Warming-Up

Warming up the body before strenuous exercise is a must if you want to get the most out of your training and avoid injury.

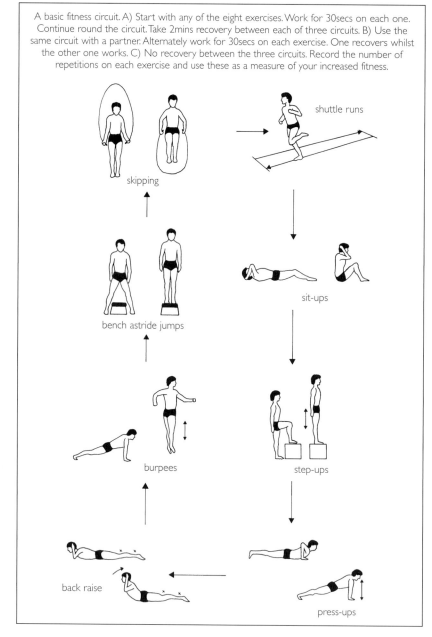

A basic fitness circuit. A) Start with any of the eight exercises. Work for 30secs on each one. Continue round the circuit. Take 2mins recovery between each of three circuits. B) Use the same circuit with a partner. Alternately work for 30secs on each exercise. One recovers whilst the other one works. C) No recovery between the three circuits. Record the number of repetitions on each exercise and use these as a measure of your increased fitness.

skipping

shuttle runs

bench astride jumps

sit-ups

burpees

step-ups

back raise

press-ups

A basic fitness circuit. Start with any of the eight exercises. Work for 30sec on each one. Repeat the circuit three times.

At a minimum, use the first part of a run to gear the heart and lungs into action and warm the muscles. Do this for 5–10min. If you are doing an interval or hard session, it is worth doing a more specific warm-up, mixing aerobic exercise, some dynamic stretches, running drills and some faster runs.

Refer to the examples in Chapter 9 to select a specific warm-up.

Cooling Down

Cooling down is also important. If you have been for a run, take the last couple of minutes to slow down and relax. If you have done some intervals, run steadily for a few minutes after you have finished. If you have tight muscles, do a little stretching on these while you are still warm or after you get home.

Pulse Count as a Measure of Fitness

Think about it. If you make the body improve the way it transports and utilizes oxygen through training, it won't need so much oxygen for you just to stand still. So as you get fitter, your resting heart rate goes down. If you want to use this theory, then take your pulse rate every morning before you get up or after 20min lying down. Count for 15sec and multiply by four. If your resting pulse starts to go up, this could be a sign of tiredness or overtraining.

Another measure of increased fitness is the rate of recovery between or after hard efforts or intervals. Take your pulse after you have warmed up to give you a 'base rate', then take your pulse at the end of a hard run or interval and again every minute. How long does it take to return to base rate? As you become fitter, this recovery time will be reduced. Some serious runners will train with a heart rate monitor strapped to them. This enables every session to be performed at the right effort and maximizes training time.

Running Training Stage 2

Your next goals are two-fold. The first is to make one of your weekly runs short but fast; the other is to make another of your weekly runs longer. For the fast one, plan a route that takes 25–30min. Use the first 5–10min to get warmed up, then run the rest of the route as fast as you can. If you like using the same route, set a watch on it from the end of the warm-up point and treat it as a time trial. Remember to add a jog recovery to cool down. The long run goal should be to increase the run gradually to twice the length of time you expect to be out on an average orienteering course. You are now seriously training and should be feeling the many benefits.

Do you want to move on? You are gaining speed and endurance, now you need some strength to run up the hills and give your running some power. So, run up some hills! Try to choose hilly routes especially for your long run and put in some extra effort as you run up. Hill intervals will more specifically develop leg strength. Choose a hill with a gradient you can run up. Start with ten times 20sec sprints up and recover as you walk down. Next time you go out, do two sets of six, with 5min to recover between each set, then add on one or two sprints until you reach two sets of ten.

Circuit training is another way to develop strength as well as endurance and regular core stability exercises are worth considering now that you are developing a training regime.

So far, all the training is aerobic; the runs should have different intensities but are always comfortable and you should be able to talk while doing them.

Core Stability

Your core muscles (abdominal and lower back) act as stabilizers for everyday activities as well as sports. The aim of core stability training is effectively to recruit the trunk musculature; by strengthening these muscles the body is helped to hold a good posture, which has benefits for running style and basic endurance. This is one of many extra sessions you can add to improve your fitness. Details of core stability can be found on one of the sports coach or running training websites.

Plyometric Training

Plyometrics is a type of exercise training designed to produce fast, powerful movements. In orienteering, a fast, powerful running style is needed for speedy traversing through undulating terrain. Imagine yourself running through heather or marshy ground; in these situations you need leg power to lift your knees up to run over the ground rather than get sucked in by it. The legs work explosively and it is this quality that is sought after through plyometrics. Jumping, hopping and bounding type exercises are plyometrics that are incorporated into many fitness circuits. Examples of this would be squat jumps or bench jumps.

Specific plyometric running sessions can also be incorporated into your training. High-intensity bounding intervals are one of the most beneficial for orienteers training hard for national or international recognition. If you decide to introduce bounding into your training, watch out for muscle strain; only do so after a period of good basic training and limit it to forty to sixty foot strikes per session to start with.

BASIC FITNESS SESSIONS

Plan to do three or four of these each week:

- easy aerobic run
- fast medium-intensity run of 20–30min
- long run up to twice your orienteering time
- short hill intervals for leg strength
- gym or circuit session
- core stability
- orienteering event.

Running Training Stage 3

If you have reached this stage in your training, I would recommend that you put some thought into making a periodized programme (see Chapter 12). If this

Long runs over moorland are good for strength and endurance.

doesn't appeal or suit your lifestyle, then just read more about different types of training included in Chapter 12, selecting sessions linked to your major events. Try to introduce some variety into your training. This could be cross-training (different sports with similar fitness demands), or a variety of terrain. Long runs over marshy and heather moorland are good for strength, as well as testing determination and a positive attitude.

Keeping a Training Diary

If training has become part of your life, you should write it all down. Doing this supports motivation in a similar way to reporting to a coach. You can buy an orienteering training diary, or log your training in a notebook or electronically. One main purpose of doing this is to prevent over-training. You should plan in easy and rest weeks throughout the year. Some people like to record their training as distance and aim for so many miles or kilometres each week, while others prefer time. It's up to you. If you are following a year plan, then a training log is your source of information from which to progress. Use it to plan the next year's programme, avoiding increasing the quantity in each phase by more than 10 per cent.

TRAINING LOGS

Training logs should include the following headings:

- training phase
- day
- waking pulse
- type of training
- quality – easy/moderate/hard/ maximum
- daily and total distance
- daily and total time
- hours of sleep
- comments
- days ill or injured
- how you feel
- new shoes

Over-Training

If your training log shows a gradual increase in time and distance each week without any breaks for more than four weeks then you are asking for trouble. General tiredness, being unable to sleep, running times becoming worse rather than better and injury are all indications of over-training.

Orienteering demands flexibility and agility in forested and rough terrain.

1. get a book or diary to record all your training
2. decide if you want a coach or can manage on your own
3. have a plan.

Work through this section with a notebook and diary, gradually building up your plan.

Select your Goals

Do you have a long-term ambition, such as running for Britain in five years' time or winning a Masters race in two years? To achieve long-term goals you will need specific goals for each year beforehand. First, which race or races will be your main goal for this year? These will be your focus over the year and influence the type of training suited to being in top form on the days of those races. Discuss your ambitions and ideas with your coach, friend or parent. Be realistic on the one hand, but having a dream of being a champion can be exceedingly motivating and gives you drive to train hard through the winter and periods of other commitments and work.

In summary, start your training plan with:

• your main future long-term goal
• this year's goal
• events that are most important to you
• other events that will be good training.

Design and draw up a table with months and weeks for a year, so that you can map out your year's plan. The examples below will be used to illustrate each part of the plan. If you are under 16 or new to training, use Goal 1 as a guide.

Goal Setting

Goal 1 To achieve a top five place in the local colour-coded league by focusing on five out of the eight events.

Goal 2 To aim to be selected for a British summer training tour or an International in July. Good performances needed in the named seven selection races.

Goal 3 To aim to be a British Champion and perform well at a summer multiday event.

Competition Phase

I would start with the competition phase and work the year plan from here. You are creating one or more competition phases that are the base for the rest of your training plan. This period should not extend for more than ten weeks, as it is difficult to maintain physical and psychological form for longer than this. If you want to race throughout the year, pick out the events in which you would want to perform best and use the others for rehearsal and training. Each competition phase should start one or two weeks before the first race to allow for recovery from hard specific training. Let's have a look at the plan so far with the races put in.

Goal 1 In Goal 1, with the eight events spread though the year, I have chosen to have two competition periods using the two early events for practice and gauging whether the goal is realistic. The last event should be fine after reaching good fitness for the autumn races, aiming for good focus on the day.

Goal 2 The next example shows a classic British racing period in April and May. All the races are equally important.

Goal 1	Jan	Feb	Mar	Apr	May	Jun	Jul	Aug	Sep	Oct	Nov	Dec
weeks												

The competition phase. The red cells show weeks with one to five races at the end of that week.
Goal 1: to achieve a top five place in the local colour-coded series – six out of eight events.

Goal 2	Jan	Feb	Mar	Apr	May	Jun	Jul	Aug	Sep	Oct	Nov	Dec
weeks												

Goal 2: to be selected for a British summer training tour or a July international. Good performances in the seven selection races and good fitness in July are required.

Goal 3	Jan	Feb	Mar	Apr	May	Jun	Jul	Aug	Sep	Oct	Nov	Dec
weeks												

Goal 3: to become British Champion and perform well at a summer multiday event.

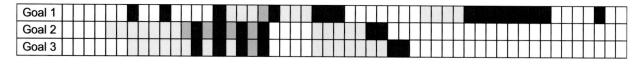

The specific training phases are added to the competition weeks.

	Jan	Feb	Mar	Apr	May	Jun	Jul	Aug	Sep	Oct	Nov	Dec
Goal 1						R						R
Goal 2					R		R					
Goal 3					R		R					

The whole year plan with basic training and recovery weeks added; r = rehearsal race.

Goal 3 The British Championships is shown in May on the example. Other races will be important preparation, but will be brought into the specific training phase. The main mental focus and preparation is on the one race.

Specific Training Phase

This phase runs for four to six weeks before the main races. It is important because it specifically prepares you for reaching peak fitness and readiness for the orienteering races. It should include some races to practise techniques and racing strategies. If you have a series of races that are monthly, your basic fitness should come before any specific training. Follow the plan for Goal 1 to see how this works.

Basic Training Phase

The total distance and time spent in this phase is the base from which you will race. The period can be as long as eighteen weeks, or as short as four. It can also be combined with more specific training if the total time for race preparation is limited to six weeks or less. It is also good to include other aerobic sports such as swimming, cycling, fell running, mountaineering, ski touring or ski racing. These can increase your enjoyment of training and help to prevent injury because the stresses are varied.

Transition and Recovery Phase

'R' in the examples represents a period of active recovery where you can give yourself a deserved break after racing hard. It is also a relaxing transition between a competition phase and the next period of race preparation.

Planning the Weeks

You should be able to see your life panning out before you for at least the next eight to ten months. Now is the time to see if you can fit your training into your available time.

Hard and Easy weeks

Start by adding your easy, medium and hard weeks to the plan. This weekly pattern helps you to recover and avoid overtraining. It also helps you to fit your training alongside education, work, holidays and other time commitments.

Do the easy weeks first. Go through the whole year, week by week and mark 'E' against all the enforced easy weeks. These would include the week before a major race, holidays or periods away involving other activities, examinations or intense work weeks and weeks that involve travelling for one full day or more.

The medium (M) and hard (H) weeks are then slotted in according to preference. You can choose an easy–hard

> **EASY WEEKS**
>
> A summary of the easy weeks is:
>
> - the week before a major race
> - holidays or periods away involving other activities
> - examination or intense work weeks
> - weeks that involve a day or more travelling.

cycle, or an easy–medium–hard cycle. It doesn't matter if you have to break the pattern and even have two or three easy weeks together. This is how life is. Be pleased with the final result; it is your plan.

This is the place to offer the alternative of a four-week cycle, which many athletes would recommend. The pattern here is easy, medium, hard, rest. The chance of a week off every month could fit into your lifestyle better. Now is the time to decide which cycle to opt for.

As you fill in the details, you will see that an easy week in one phase will not necessarily be the same as an easy week in a later one. You will also note that in the basic training phase both the easy and hard weeks will increase in quantity as the phase progresses. The last hard week in the basic training phase should be the one with the greatest distance or quantity of training of any week in any of the four phases in the competition year.

CHAPTER 12

PERIODIZATION

Developing a Periodized Training Programme

Once you have reached a good level of basic fitness and still want to improve your orienteering speed, consider progressing to planning your own periodized programme.

The section which follows shows you how to plan a periodized programme designed to give you optimum fitness for the races you want to run well in. Your best form will be gained after a period of intensive quality training. This can only be coped with once a high level of basic fitness has been achieved. The period of basic training, therefore, aims to raise your aerobic capacity, which serves to increase the efficiency of the oxygen transport system. The body is then able to handle the stresses of hard-quality training sessions designed to increase speed, strength and endurance for orienteering. Your plan will contain four phases:

1. basic fitness training phase
2. specific fitness and orienteering technique training phase
3. competition phase
4. transition and recovery phase.

If you decide to start training there are a number of things you need to do first:

STARTING OUT

If you are under 16 or new to training:

- concentrate on basic fitness
- only include specific training under coach guidance
- make sure you think it is worthwhile
- use Goal 1 (see next page) as a guide.

Once you have reached a good level of basic fitness and still want to improve your orienteering speed, consider planning a periodized training programme.

Flexibility, Agility and Mobility

The nature of orienteering demands a huge amount of flexibility and agility in forested and rough terrain. Ducking under or leaping over fallen trees, negotiating felled or low-visibility areas, scrambling down cliffs or steep rocky ground are examples of where good body management helps to maintain the flow of running and saves energy required for running fast and thinking fast.

Flexibility exercises should become part of a well-planned training programme. Join a yoga class or do some regular static stretching exercises. These contribute to improved flexibility and should be practised as a separate session. They are very beneficial after hard training, when the muscles can tighten and stiffen. Mobility and agility can be improved by doing a regular general fitness circuit such as that shown earlier in this chapter. You could even set up your own obstacle course outside with obstacles to leap over, roll under, and squeeze through like a mini-assault course. Developing core stability contributes to good agility and terrain running style.

Training and Lifestyle

Keeping fit, whatever way you do it, will contribute to being healthy. The body is designed to be active and like any engine it requires good care and attention: if it's cold and wet, wear appropriate clothing; shower and change as soon as possible after the run and think how good you feel once you are back at home. Running is cheap and it helps to make you look good. Find the best weight where you feel 'right', can run hard and don't feel dizzy after a bath. Being underweight is as bad as being overweight. Extra carbohydrate is necessary to keep a committed runner happy.

If you are training hard and have a full-time job, management of your plan is essential if you are going to avoid stress and be a sociable member of your family. At the beginning of each week I check my work diary first, see if there are any other commitments, then plan what training session to do each day and at what time. Doing what you have planned reinforces motivation and confidence.

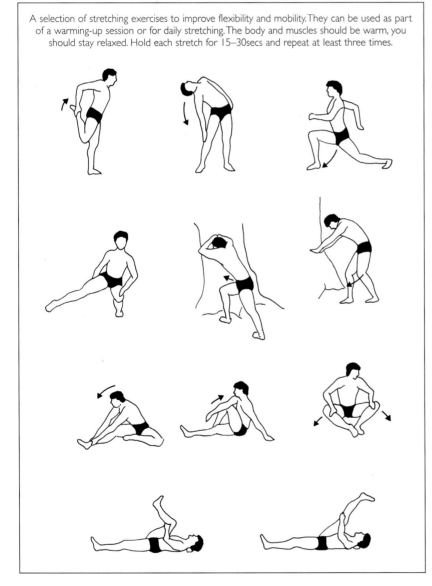

A selection of stretching exercises to improve flexibility and mobility. They can be used as part of a warming-up session or for daily stretching. The body and muscles should be warm, you should stay relaxed. Hold each stretch for 15–30secs and repeat at least three times.

A selection of static stretching exercises to improve flexibility and mobility. Make this a daily routine. Hold each stretch for 15–30sec and repeat three times on each side.

TRAINING TIPS

Avoid the following:

- illness and injury
- over-training
- too much road running
- cheap running shoes
- poor diet
- lack of sleep
- hanging around in damp clothes.

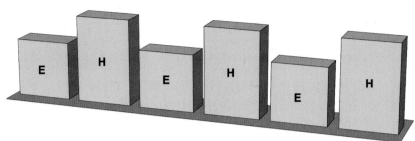

A two-week cycle of easy–hard training.

To decide the quantity of this hardest week, you must first ask yourself what is the furthest distance you have comfortably run in one week. Add 10 per cent to this figure to give you the distance to put in the plan. For each of the hard weeks prior to that, subtract between 5 and 10km, or 3 to 6 miles. You should now see the pattern developing, with the quantity of training gradually building up to the peak. Afterwards, the distance gradually decreases, ith all the weeks becoming proportionately shorter as more intensive work is included in the specific training phase. Eventually, you ease off completely for the races in which you are aiming to peak.

In this table, using the first goal as an example, the hardest distance week in the basic training phase is 40 miles/kilometres (your choice), but the actual physically hardest week is the last week in April because it includes quality training sessions as well as basic distance. If you refer to the quality and quantity graph, this hardest

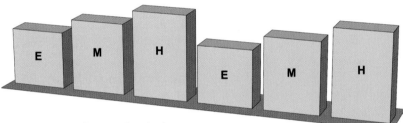

A three-week cycle of easy–medium–hard training.

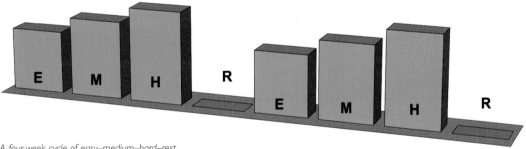

A four-week cycle of easy–medium–hard–rest.

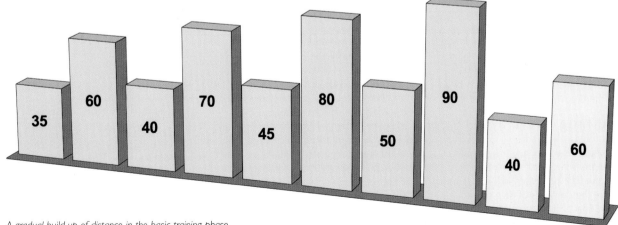

A gradual build-up of distance in the basic training phase.

Goal 1	Jan			Feb			Mar			Apr			May			Jun		
phase	basic			■		■	basic			spec			spec			com		R
1st easy				E		E				E			E	E				
E/M/H	E	H	E	H	E	H		H	M		M	H	E	H		H	E	H			M	H	E	H	M
Km/miles	10	15	12	20	14	25	12	30	15	12	20	35	15	**40**	10	20	15	**25**	14	12	15	20	14	20	15	12

Planning the weeks. Goal 1 for six months. Start with the enforced easy weeks. Follow this with fitting in the easy, medium and hard weeks. Finally, add distance starting with the highest of 40 (in this example) at the end of the basic training phase.

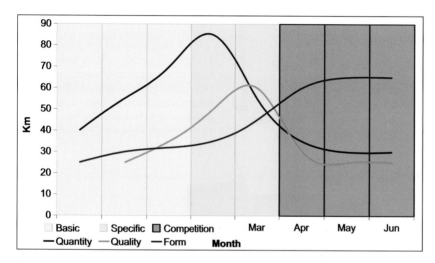

The balance of quantity and quality training in the competition year. Top form is reached for this competition phase in April and May.

only a guide; you can adapt it to suit your lifestyle, goals and motivation to train.

The Training Phases

Basic Fitness Training Phase

The aim here is to develop endurance in order to cope with the load of specific training and the races that follow. This basic fitness is an essential part of the periodized year. If you have just started training, refer to the advice given in Chapter 11 under running training stages one and two. If you dip into the sessions shown in the table on the next page, just stick to the basic fitness

week is where the quality line meets the distance or quantity line. This is a week to plan carefully with plenty to eat and lots of sleep. The traditional Easter 'JK' (Jan Kjellstrom) races are not one of the main goals, so they have been included in the specific training phase as rehearsal or practice races.

Planning the Days

A training session or a training unit is a single practice session with a training objective. The objectives will vary as they pursue the demands of each phase.

The final part of completing your year plan is to write down the training sessions

you would include for two or three weeks of each phase – an easy week and a hard week, or an easy, medium and hard week. Refer to the table of training sessions in each phase and select five to ten sessions to make up each week. Keep in mind your target distance or time, and balance hard and easy days. If you are able to train more than once a day, ensure that you allow adequate time for recovery.

It is worth doing all this now, even though you might adjust the detail as the year progresses. You are providing a poster to stick on a wall and tick off the sessions and weeks. If you know which sessions you are going to do each week, this helps in actually getting out of the door and doing them. The information given here is

---

BASIC TRAINING PHASE

Easy week (early part), six sessions:

- long distance (LSD) 60–90min
- circuit training
- short distance (SD) 25–45min
- distance run (LSD) 40–60min
- long intervals (LI)
- rest – other activity
- long distance (LSD) 45–70min.

Hard week (later part), eight sessions:

- LSD 50–90min
- a) SD 30–45min; b) circuit
- long hill intervals (LH)
- a) LSD 30–40min; b) LSD 40–60min
- LI
- rest
- LSD in terrain 50–120min.

RECOMMENDED TRAINING SESSIONS FOR EACH PHASE

Basic Training Sessions	Specific Training Sessions	Competition Training Sessions
Long slow distance 50–120min Distance runs (LSD) 25–50min Other active sports Circuit training Core stability Running drills Orienteering events	Long slow distance Distance runs Circuit training Running drills Plyometrics Core stability Technique training	Long slow distance Distance runs Technique training
Quality	Quality	Quality
Short distance (SD) Long intervals Long hills Short hills for strength Fartlek Cross-country races Fell races	Short distance Long intervals Short intervals Long hills Bounding Short hills Hills & sprints Marsh/sand/heather intervals Fartlek Threshold runs Sub-threshold runs Special variations Weight training Specific circuits Cross-country races Fell races Road races Orienteering races Technique training	Short distance Short hills Short intervals Marsh/sand/heather intervals Special variations Fartlek Orienteering races

sessions for a year while you establish a regime that fits your lifestyle. Long runs should be done in terrain whenever possible. Use events for terrain running training, as well as practising new techniques. Analyse your races and plan your technique training for the next phase.

In the second half of this phase you will have gained enough fitness to include at least two quality sessions each week. You should find that hill sessions have an immediate effect, so put one of these in first. Short hills (10sec) with a full recovery are useful for increasing muscle strength, a

necessary element for the specific training that follows and for future races in rough terrain. Circuits are excellent for building up aerobic and specific fitness, especially over the winter period. If you decide that three or four sessions a week is all you have time for, then select your sessions with variety in mind.

Be wary of over-training in this period when you might be piling on the miles. Don't train if you feel a bit under par, or need to recover fully from an injury. If you find you have to take some time off, try to think positively about the time you have available before the major events. This phase over the winter is long, so the build-up of fitness is gradual and one or two breaks can easily be accommodated. A good diet and plenty of sleep will contribute to staying healthy and sticking to your programme.

Another way to lay out your weekly plan is shown in the example below of a week in the Basic Training Phase of an international runner.

Specific Training Phase

Here you develop fitness and racing skills specific to the demands of orienteering. This is the most demanding phase, involving

	Mon	Tue	Wed	Thurs	Fri	Sat	Sun
AM	60min medium run	35min easy run	50min medium effort run	35min easy	35min easy	20min warm up/down three × 8min (85% MHR)	90min–120min easy
PM	10 × 10sec hill sprints Core strength session	Track – eight laps, striding the straights /jogging the bends	35min easy run Core strength session	50min (70– 80% MHR)	45min medium plus strides	35min recovery run	Core strength session

SPECIFIC TRAINING PHASE

A hard week, eight sessions:

- a) short distance (SD) 30–45min
  b) circuit
- long intervals (LI)
- 'O' technique 40–70min
- fartlek 40–60min
- short hills (SH), or hills and sprints (H&S)
- long distance (LSD) 35–65min
- 'O' technique 50–70 min.

An easy week, seven sessions:

- SD 25–45min
- special variation 1
- LSD with O technique 40–60min
- SH or H&S
- special variation 2
- LSD 35–60min
- competition.

TECHNIQUE PRACTICES IN SPECIFIC TRAINING PHASE

- Techniques that need practice.
- Refine racing strategies.
- Use races to rehearse preparation routines.
- Use mental training exercises to improve concentration and build confidence.
- Look at and run with maps of the big race terrain.
- Believe that your preparation is the best it could be.

TRAINING TIPS

- Beware training overload, which results in a negative effect on fitness, illness or injury.
- Include a very easy run or rest day each week.
- Do not train if feeling unwell.
- Make sure you have plenty of carbohydrates, iron and vitamin C in your diet.

COMPETITION PHASE

Week 1 – six sessions:

- LSD terrain run with map 50–70min
- short intervals (SI)
- technique 40–60min
- short distance (SD) 25–40min
- anaerobic intervals (AI)
- rest
- competition.

Week 2 – six sessions:

- LSD 40–60min
- short hills (SH)
- technique 40–60min
- AI
- rest
- short run with fast sprints 25–40min
- competition or LSD.

TIP

Include other activities or social events while big races are on to take some pressure off needing a good result.

tempted to do hard sessions because you are feeling so fit, save yourself for the races. Record your training the week before a race so that you can repeat or modify a pattern of training that leads to a good result. Some people surprisingly find they orienteer at their best the day after a cross country or short fell race. I would translate this into a short run with fast bursts of speed to 'remind' the muscles how to work. If your competition phase covers several weeks then fit in a harder week to improve or maintain sharpness when there isn't a major race to ease up for. Thorough analysis of races is important for future planning.

Once again, if you are new to training select three or four aerobic sessions from either of these weeks.

Recovery and Transition Phase

If you are aspiring to be a top orienteer this phase should consist of active recovery. You need to give your brain a rest from orienteering, take away any pressure of races and revive your

the sharpening of fitness and increase of oxygen uptake capacity. Remember that this cannot take place without the preceding work on basic training. Your weekly mileage drops as you include at least three quality sessions. Technique work should be thorough and focused on honing race skills and all techniques. Those relatively new to training should stick to three or four sessions a week, but now include some intervals; I would recommend you try the hills and sprints first (H&S).

Competition Phase

The races in this period are what you have been training for. You should be looking forward to them. All this preparation should give you confidence, an important element in performing your best. Keep focused even though you have reduced your training load. The quantity and quality of your training tapers down so your body adapts and finds its best form. Do not be

Recovery and transition phases. Be active, but do something different.

motivation for achieving future goals. This is the time to review your performances and plan next year's programme. Have a holiday, go cycling or mountaineering. Be active, but do something different. If you want to do some training make the runs easy and relaxed.

Types of Training Used in the Different Phases

An enormous amount of information is available about training and sessions to improve speed, strength and endurance. Check out websites if you are interested in finding out more. Often the same session label will be used differently by different people. Here I expand on the terminology I have used in my outlook on periodization for orienteering. Sometimes I use time as a session base, other times I use distance. You can choose which feels best for you.

Pace and Heart Rate

Slow and fast are linked to your heart rate as a percentage of maximum. You can find out your maximum heart rate by doing a treadmill or ergocycle test with a fitness trainer or coach. Maximum heart rate (MHR) can also be achieved running up a long hill for at least 3min as hard as you can. Your heart rate at the top will be very close to your maximum. You can also use the formula: MHR = 220 minus age, which will give you a rough guide. Slow or steady state is 60–70 per cent of MHR; simply this is being able to talk while you run. Fast is aerobic, working at 70–80 per cent of MHR, where you are breathing really hard but still running below your 'anaerobic threshold'. Maximum effort is anaerobic, which is 80–90 per cent of MHR and is where you finish an interval feeling you just can't do any more (on your knees gasping for oxygen). Threshold runs are around 85 per cent MHR, where you run at your anaerobic threshold. More than this is maximum effort, which you would use for anaerobic intervals. Training

with a heart rate monitor helps in measuring the right effort more precisely.

LSD – long slow distance This is running for up to twice race time with a steady heart rate (60–70 per cent of MHR). To prevent injury, it is best done off-road. It trains basic endurance and the body gets used to working for a long time.

SD or SFD – short fast distance This is continuous fast running for up to race time, for example cross-country races, fell races and time trials. I have a set route I use as a time trial, which is also a test of improved fitness. It trains speed and endurance. These are SD: 30–60min at 70–80 per cent (sub-threshold), or SFD 20–30min at 85 per cent (threshold).

LI – long intervals (aerobic) Run fast for 2–3½min, with 1½–3min recovery. Follow this for one to two sets of three to eight repetitions, keeping equal intensity for each run. Repeat over a set circuit or as part of a continuous run.

I did a session of 8 × 3min, with 2min recovery. The route crossed marsh and heather tussocks.

SI – short intervals (aerobic) Run fast for 10–15sec with 10–15sec recovery. Repeat for two to three sets of 10–15min. These are sometimes called 15–15s. Start every 30sec. They train speed and are especially useful on sand, marsh or heather.

SH – short hills Run for 15–20sec up a steep hill using maximum effort; feel your legs working, lift your knees and keep your head up. Jog or walk back to recover. Follow this for two to three sets of eight to ten repetitions. It trains strength.

H&S – hills and sprints This session links SI with SH. Warm up by running to your steep hill (10min). Run for 20sec up a steep hill using maximum effort. Jog or walk back to recover (40sec). Repeat ten times (10min). Run to a flat path or grassy area. Sprint for 15sec with 15sec recovery. Repeat ten times (5min). It trains strength

and speed. A good session if you are short of time.

Fartlek (speed play) This is a Swedish term. The athlete is free to adjust the amount of effort and its duration on a continuous undulating run. It trains speed and endurance.

Threshold runs Also known as 'tempo' runs. These are run at your anaerobic threshold, which is around 85 per cent of your maximum and could be called 'comfortably hard'. These runs should be 20–30min with a good warm-up beforehand. See also SFD above.

Anaerobic Training

Anaerobic means 'without oxygen'. The body is challenged to work so hard that the muscles require more oxygen than can be supplied directly from the lungs and heart. An 'oxygen debt' is accumulated together with lactic acid, a waste product which builds up in the muscles and prevents them functioning fully. This also affects decision making capacity so avoid critical route choice decisions after running really hard such as at the top of steep hills. Anaerobic training challenges the body to utilize the oxygen available; by 'remembering' this there is a beneficial training effect of improving the 'anaerobic threshold' so that you can run harder for longer and when you ease off your recovery rate improves so that you can run fast again earlier and think clearly if you are orienteering.

VO_2 max Your VO_2 max is a scientific measurement related to your capacity to use oxygen at the very limit of your efforts. It is also related to age, body weight and gender. A training programme would aim to increase your VO_2 max to enable you to run harder, faster and longer in the competition phase.

AI – anaerobic intervals Run for 1–3min using maximum effort, with 2–5min rest. Repeat for three to six repetitions only. It trains speed and endurance and improves recovery rates after hard efforts in a race.

LH – long hill intervals (anaerobic) Run for 50–90sec at maximum speed up a gradual hill. Jog back for recovery. Follow this for two sets of two to four repetitions. It trains speed, strength and endurance and improves recovery rates.

VO$_2$ max intervals Run for 2–5min using maximum effort followed by equal or shorter time recovery.

Variations to Develop Speed for Orienteering

These personal favourites are sessions that have adapted training theory to the specific demands of orienteering, in which the running efforts are variable throughout each race:

• Find a 1km easy path circuit. Put out four tapes in a circuit, one every 250m. Warm up on one circuit while you put out or check the tapes. Then: run one 250m section fast, one slow, two fast; one slow, three fast; one slow, two fast, one slow; one fast, one slow. Finish with one circuit to warm down. How many kilometres have you run?

• Plan an 8–13km run along paths and tracks. Take the first 10min to warm up with easy running (not getting out of breath). Then: running and counting double paces all the time, follow this pyramid sequence:

  • fifty fast, twenty slow; twenty fast, twenty slow
  • 100 fast, twenty slow; twenty fast, twenty slow
  • 150 fast, twenty slow; twenty fast, twenty slow.

Follow this pattern up to 300 fast, then back down to fifty fast. Finish with a 10–15min warm-down jog.

• An alternative hills and sprints (H&S) session: a 30sec hill followed by a 30sec hard run off the top. Jog down for recovery; times five, build up to three sets.

Logging Your Training

This has been mentioned earlier, but it is worth repeating. You need to record what you have done and how much of it. There is no point having a plan if you don't know whether you have followed it or not. For visually oriented people it can be satisfying to create graphs of accumulated training, which can be done electronically using special software. How you record is up to you, but the final log will serve as a base for the following year's plans.

The body is challenged to work so hard that the muscles require more oxygen than can be supplied directly from the lungs and heart.

CHAPTER 13

TECHNICAL TRAINING

I would say that most orienteers put more effort into physical training and leave technical training to be covered at events. Can you imagine this working for a Wimbledon tennis player? 'I'm really fit but still having a problem with my serve, I'll work on it in my next match.' No, I don't think so. A balance is needed between practising techniques until they are completely sound and giving the mind a rest. Decide how much time you are going to set aside for technical training during the year. This can be in a build-up to major events, or in each phase of a periodized plan. You should, of course, use events that aren't important to practise weaknesses that have become evident through event analysis.

Race Analysis

In Chapter 7 advice was offered on race analysis. If you don't do any other training, the first step to improvement is to draw in your route on the map and compare this with your split times with other athletes. Race analysis gives you the information needed to identify strengths and weaknesses. These can be summed up in two categories: techniques and racing skills. Can you separate them and identify in detail exactly what it is you need to practise? Make a plan similar to the one described next and identify what skills you can practise at events and what techniques need to be practised separately. If there is an accessible permanent course, can you use this to rehearse skills or strategies?

It is worth practising techniques until they are completely sound.

Extract from a Personal Technique Training Plan

Goal
• To orienteer with confidence and gain a high placing at the British Championships on wooded sand dune terrain.
  Preparation + success = confidence.

Aims

- To apply the appropriate strategy for each control: select an attack point. Use map, compass and pacing. Identify the major features. Have a clear visualization of map to ground. Know the control description. Know my limit for estimating distance accurately.
- To maximize eyesight to see what is on the map in the shortest time.
- To change focus between green and white areas. Know when to walk and when to run.

Practice Events on Sand Dunes

- Keep speed up moving through very complex terrain.
- Look out for steep and large hills with three contours or more.
- Experiment where using a magnifier is easy and beneficial.
- Identify where pacing works best, such as where the ground flattens.
- Micro-route choice makes a difference to running rhythm; practise looking ahead.

Specific Technique Practices

- Start slow and easy, developing to fast and technical.
- Pacing practices at different distances.
- Line on a map – talk through what features are coming up. Keep looking at the map, but practice map memory for up to 100m.
- Compass and pacing with map. Pick up large features in complex terrain. Pick up smaller features in complex terrain. 'Silly' long legs. Star exercise.
- Relocation practise. 'Follow John'. Run without looking at the map for 1–5min, then relocate.
- Contours – check out 2.5m contours. What do they look like?

Interim Evaluation (Four Weeks Before Event)

- Pacing. 100m fine, 200m needs practice, 300m probably too far without map contact.
- Magnifier lens better than no lens. Use on first finger. Use for short legs and approaching controls.
- More relocation practice needed.

Using Permanent Courses

Most permanent orienteering courses (POC) have a variety of control sites at different technical levels. Once you have a map of a POC, you can decide the best way to use it for practice.

Training at Low-Key Events

Techniques or Racing Skills

Which techniques can you practise at an event and which would be better practised at a separate technique training session? How are your racing skills, such as route choice decisions and control flow? Next time you go to a race to practise a skill, check out the sort of terrain and try to get hold of a map of the area. Read Chapter 10 and decide which skills are most appropriate for the type of terrain. Select one that requires practice. This will be your focus for that event. The result should not matter. Visualize yourself performing the skill before the start and try not to be distracted from it as you race.

Using a Course with a Lower Technical Level

If you need to practise techniques such as pacing or control flow, consider entering a course at a lower standard. If you normally run Light Green (TD4) or Green (TD5), enter the Orange (TD3) and use the path

system and easier routes to practise these skills. Similarly, if you normally run Orange, enter the Yellow. Having an easier course enables you to focus more on using these skills in a race environment. Another way to use these events is to run two courses. Start with an easy course to put a newly learnt technique into practice, then enter your usual one (harder) in order to practise the same technique. These are the sort of events where you could be shadowed or go round with a friend to practise relocation or discuss routes. If you think this is a good idea, always check with the event organizer and offer to be non-competitive. After all, it is the practice that is of most importance.

Major Race Simulation

As the day of your big event comes closer, use other events to practise your warm-up and pre-start routines. Enter races of similar length, on similar terrain, at the same time of day and in different weather conditions. If you have a big event over two or three days, find another two-day event in the month beforehand, or simulate this with local events and training. All these events should be slotted into your training programme and will contribute to the growing confidence that develops from thorough preparation. Remember the four Cs: commitment leads to confidence, which enables good concentration and control of focus.

Technical Training Sessions

Setting up your own technique exercises is difficult and probably the main reason why technical training takes a low priority in people's training plans. This is where regular coaching sessions organized by your local club become so valuable and having your own coach is a benefit worth chasing. Ask one of the club coaches or someone who is an experienced orienteer to 'shadow' you round a course. This is when you will get the best feedback and

---

SKILLS PRACTICE

Use low-key events to practise:

- pre-start routine
- walking to the first control
- focusing on weak techniques
- racing skills and strategies
- racing in the same terrain as a major event
- being shadowed
- running two courses.

be given advice on which skills you need to practise. If you do have access to orienteering terrain, you will have a better chance of making a thorough technique training plan alongside your physical training.

Making a Technique Training Plan

Using a copy of the check chart, look at the list of race skills and give yourself a score out of ten for each line. This immediately shows you weaker skills that need practice. Then, using events and technique sessions, be systematic in working through the list, ticking off each skill or technique as you work on it. Before your big races or competition phase, you need at least three to four ticks against your best skills to make them even better and five to twenty ticks against your weaknesses. Score yourself again periodically to mark improvements. Colour-code your good, medium and poor skills, or change the order on file.

Technique Exercises

Here are some exercises that are straightforward to set up and don't need controls. They can all be planned and adapted to suit every level of ability. Some of them are also used as practice tasks in previous chapters.

Map reading – line orienteering This is done individually or in pairs. Draw a line on the map that is about 1–2km in length, linking features that you are able to find and follow. Follow the line as accurately as possible. Alternate the lead if you are in a pair. This also trains map memory; look at the line and see how far you can follow it before you have to look at the map again. Lines which weave around a lot should be kept short as they require a lot of concentration.

Map reading – contour only Ask your club map printer if you can have a contour-only map of an area you would be allowed to train in. Plan a line or a course with control features to find.

Relocation – 'Follow John' In pairs; one runner leads the way reading the map, then stops beside a distinct feature. The second runner relocates, agrees the location, then takes the lead and repeats the exercise. The following runner chooses to look at the

Use low-key events to be shadowed.

Line orienteering. Trains map reading and map memory. Follow the line as accurately as possible.

TECHNIQUE AND RACE-TRAINING CHECK CHART

Score out of ten for each skill/technique (ten is good practice, one is pretty awful).

Year: Goal:	Date: marks out of ten	Tick every time you practice	Date: marks out of ten	More practice	Score
Running and orienteering					
Choosing routes					
Estimating difficulty of legs					
Hitting first control					
Selecting attack points					
Following a route plan					
Attacking controls					
Control flow					
Running in rough terrain					
Checking control codes					
Reading descriptions					
Fine map reading					
Rough map reading					
Reading contours					
Using the compass					
Distance judgement					
Relocation					
Concentration					
Running independently					
Distracted by others					
Distracted by other controls					
Controlling pre-race nerves					
Ability to relax					
Fear of failing/not achieving race goal (4 to 6 best)					
Need to achieve (8 out of 10 best)					
Self-belief (to achieve goals)					

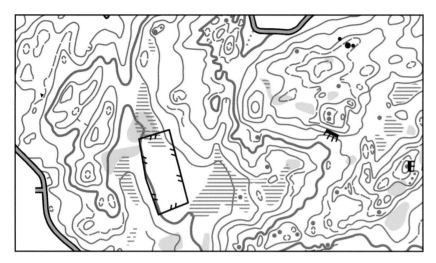

Contour only. Trains map reading. Plan a line or a course to follow.

Map section	Distance	Double paces running
1	100m	43
2	100m	40
3	150m	62
4	100m	43
5	400m	158
6	400m	155
7	100m	38
8	50m	21
Total	1,400m	560

map while following, or only when they have stopped to change the lead.

Compass bearings 1 – running on the needle Choose an area with lots of criss-crossing paths and plan a route to cut across the blocks of woodland, aiming for path junctions. See how close you can get to each junction by just following the compass. This is a chance to notice if you have a left or right bias.

Compass bearings 2 – aiming off Using a similar area to the above, plan a route to cut across the blocks so as to aim off for the junctions. You should be able to run faster than trying to hit each junction exactly.

Compass bearings 3 – on slopes It is useful to know if you have a tendency to under-compensate or over-compensate for the slope when following a bearing downhill. Practise in an appropriate area to test your accuracy.

Pace counting Plan a short route along paths. Mark the map at junctions, then measure and number each section. Run the circuit counting double paces, writing down the number of paces taken for each section. Add up the total distance and paces, then work out an average running pace for 100m on tracks and paths. When you have an average pace count plan a path run to test it out, measuring and counting as you go. Repeat the exercise walking to find your average walking pace. In the table the total double paces is divided by fourteen to give an average of forty double running paces to 100m.

Map reading – attack point into control Star exercise interval session. Plan a star exercise of six to ten controls in an area that requires good map reading.

Compass bearings on slopes. Test your accuracy in an area like this.

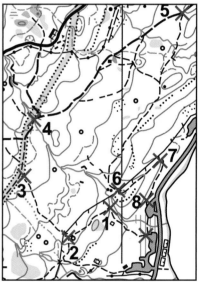

Pace counting. Run the circuit counting and recording paces for each section.

Keep the controls within 200m of the base. Take some tapes to put out at the sites. Start at the base, take a tape and, treating the base as your attack point, use map and compass carefully to find your first control site. Hang the tape, then sprint back to base as fast as possible. Repeat this with all the control sites. It takes quite a lot of care, as you are finding the site without a control there to confirm you are in the right place. Then repeat the exercise to bring in each tape, this time running faster on compass to find each tape; with a short

---

TECHNICAL TRAINING SESSIONS

Technical training sessions:

- train on orienteering terrain (with a map)
- follow a line pre-marked on a map
- plan a route to cut corners with compass bearings
- run on compass bearings to hit obvious junctions
- practise counting paces on pre-measured sections
- plan a star exercise and use as an interval session.

Indoor technique training:

- map memory exercises
- map games
- link games with a fitness circuit.

Other ideas for technique training:

- make a map
- plan some courses.

---

recovery from untying the tape, run as fast as possible back.

Orienteering Map Games

Map games are good fun and an enjoyable way of learning more about orienteering. They can be played sitting down, or running, as an individual, pair or part of a team. Following are a few favourites.

Map jigsaws   Paste the maps onto card and cut into various shapes or sizes. Make up

again with or without the original map. Do it on a table or as part of a running game, making the map up at the opposite end of a hall or field carrying one piece at a time.

Matching maps   You will need two copies of the same map for this game. Cut out identical pieces from each map and make up two sets of eight. Large pieces are

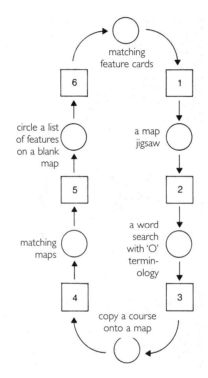

An orienteering circuit. Select six exercises from the basic fitness circuit in Chapter 11 and include a map game between each exercise. Allow 30sec for each game or exercise. Drawing games will need a map for each person.

easy; small pieces hard. Paste one set onto card and number one to eight. Use different-coloured card for the second set and letter them A to H in a different order. Match numbers with letters on one spot or as a running game. This game can also be played like the memory game Pelmanism. Mix up the two sets of maps upside-down on a table. Each player is allowed to turn two cards up at a time. If they match, the pair of cards is kept. Who can collect the most matching pairs?

Map symbol cards   Make up two sets of cards. The first set has map symbols; the second has the names of the symbols. Mix up each set, then see how quickly you can match them all. Then put each set at opposite ends of a hall, field or hill. Run with a name, pick up the correct symbol and return. Repeat until all are matched up at the start. This is fun with teams of three or four. Select symbols appropriate to the level of participants.

Place the map on the map   Use two maps of the same area. Cut out parts of one map. Large pieces will be easy; small pieces hard; simple, large-scale maps easy; small-scale complex areas hard. Time yourself or teams to place one piece at a time on the whole map. This can also be done by map memory of the piece and circling the correct area on the whole map.

Remember the course   Put one blank map at one end of an indoor or outdoor area, the same map with a course on at the other. Start with the start triangle, then work round the course one control at a time. You look at the control circle;

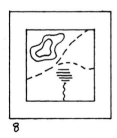 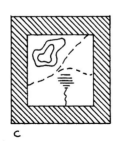

Matching maps.

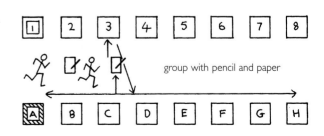

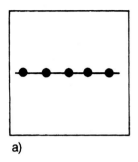

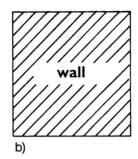

a)   b)   c)

Map symbol cards. Make two sets of cards, one set with feature symbols and one set with feature names.

remember where it is, then draw it on the other map. Alternatively, work in pairs; you remember then describe the control to your partner, who then puts the circle on the map.

Contour-only colouring Use a large-scale, contour-only map of a complex area with lots of features on. How many hilltops can you find in 2min? Colour them in and count. How many re-entrants can you find? Draw a red line down the middle of each re-entrant.

Orienteering Donkey Instead of a donkey on the wall and a pin in a tail, use a simple large contour map and contour features as labels. In pairs, one blindfolded

with the label, the other tells the blindfolded partner where to put the label on the map. Swap over for the next label. Use hilltop, spur, re-entrant, steep ground, flat ground, depression and form line.

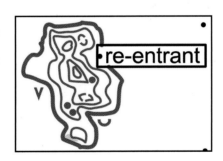

Orienteering Donkey.

Control features Have a map, or maps with several controls on; either a course or just controls like a score course. Number a list to match the number of controls. Write down what feature is in the centre of each circle. Practise with one map sitting down, then follow up by making it into a running game with another set of control sites.

Course planning Planning courses gives you an insight into how a planner sets challenges at each level of orienteering. Refer to the colour-coded course guidelines in Chapter 2. At TD5 a planner has a number of priorities and guidelines that will help to provide the best courses (see box).

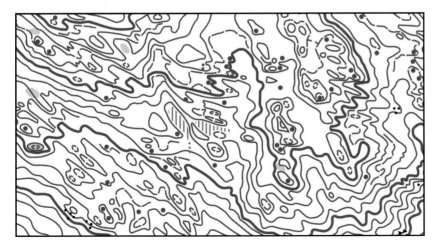

Contour-only colouring. How many hilltops? Colour them in as you count.

PLANNING PRIORITIES AND GUIDELINES FOR TD5

Following are the planning priorities and guidelines for TD5:

- map reading legs are top of the list
- route choice legs
- 'the sum of the longest two legs equals a third of the total length'
- attack points and catching features as far away from controls as possible
- offer a variety of direction, leg length, control sites and terrain type
- the control site should be on the far side of the feature
- compass and pacing legs to be avoided
- no 'bingo' or hidden controls.

CHAPTER 14

MENTAL TRAINING

When athletes get to the top of their sport, mental training and application become the key part of winning. Everyone at this level will be superbly fit with excellent map-reading skills, but dealing with the pressures and executing correct choices in a major race are skills to be managed and mastered.

Successful orienteers have the ability to focus completely on the job in hand, that is, they will know exactly where they are and where they are going, without being distracted by other people or controls they don't need to visit. The sort of concentration required to achieve this comes from being totally motivated to achieve ambitious goals. This chapter, on mental training, examines the factors that influence good concentration and deals with the problems linked with competitive anxiety.

ATTRIBUTES OF SUCCESSFUL ORIENTEERS

Successful orienteers possess the following attributes:

- set achievable goals
- are confident
- have self-belief
- have a positive attitude
- are well-prepared
- have good concentration
- are able to relax.

Goal Setting

Having race goals has been mentioned as part of preparing your training plan in Chapter 12. What does doing well in a race mean to you? You need to think through what sort of results you are capable of, as well as what would be a

---

GOALS SHOULD BE SMARTER

Specific goals
Measurable training or racing targets
Achievable goals
Realistic goals
Time-based goals and training targets
Exciting or challenging
Recorded

A dream comes true. Jamie Stevenson, World Championship gold medallist. When athletes reach the top of their sport, mental training and application becomes the key part of winning.

dream come true. To have a good result means you have orienteered well, so your goals should reflect how you are going to orienteer as well as the outcome of the race. Your goals should be SMARTER, or just SMART (see box).

So let's look at some possible goals linked to the training examples in Chapter 12.

Goal 1: to achieve a top five place in the local colour-coded series – five out of eight events

S – At each event I must focus totally on orienteering at my best.

M – I will try not to make more than three mistakes.

A – I know I am capable of being in the top five because I have done it once already.

R – If I go to all the events, I have a good chance of a top five result in at least six of them.

T – This is going to happen this year. I am going to do some sort of training three times a week.

Goal 2: selection for a British summer training tour or a July international

S – I must focus my training and orienteer at my best at each of the seven selection races.

M – I must concentrate throughout each race and avoid distraction.

A – If I look after myself, train to my plan and avoid injury I can do it.

R – I have beaten all the others in my class at least once, so I just need to orienteer well at these events.

T – If I run my time trial in X minutes I know I am fit enough to be top this year.

Goal 3: to be a British Champion; to win the British Championship in my age class

You might know that you are fitter than any of your competitors, but can you orienteer better than any of them? How you orienteer on race day is what will make you a champion or not and therefore your focus should be on orienteering as well as you can, not on beating anyone else. You can only control your performance, not anyone else's.

S – To win I must run well and focus totally on orienteering at my best.

M – I will aim to hit every control first time and if I make a mistake stay calm and refocus.

A – To be within 5min of first would be fine; within 10min not so good.

R – To win is my dream, but I'd be happy with a top five place; top 10 okay, but I can do better than that.

T – I will train to run my race distance in X minutes as a measure of fitness.

Confidence

Confidence develops over time and is needed to achieve the performance you are aiming for. How do you get it? Well, start by believing that you can do it! If you think you can race well, you are more likely to be successful. If you are going to worry about making mistakes, then you probably will. Self-belief contributes to all winning performances. Next, check your attitude – is it positive or negative? To be confident, you must believe that you are in control of your destiny. People who put themselves down, or have a habit of blaming their mistakes on other things instead of themselves, aren't going to achieve a lot. It helps if your cup is half full, rather than half empty.

Confidence also comes with good preparation, having a plan and following it. If you become ill or injured re-plan in a positive, optimistic way and be pleased with your revised goals. Try to avoid going down the negative 'it's all gone wrong, I can't do anything right' route.

Confidence = good concentration = chance of success.

Fragility of Confidence

When you are racing, losing confidence can happen in a flash; a small mistake, a slight loss of concentration and it has gone. To recover, bring back your focus to where you are and what you are going to do next. To regain confidence, you need to get back into the race with a positive attitude.

Relay winners. To win we must run well and focus totally on orienteering at our best.

Concentration

I sometimes compare the concentration needed for racing to being totally absorbed in a good book. You are in it, unaware of fire, police or ambulance events going on around you – or even a call for tea. Can you recall this kind of experience? This is the state you should be in during the orienteering races you want to do well in. Some call it 'relaxed concentration', others 'control of focus', or just 'the X factor' – you can't just turn it on; it just happens and it feels like luck is on your side.

SOME DEMONS OF CONCENTRATION

These can seriously affect concentration:

- low confidence
- high anxiety
- too great a fear of failing
- negative thoughts
- too great a dependency on success
- making a mistake
- distraction by others.

But as you work your way up the leader board it is quite probable that you will come across all the demons that are trying to distract you from achieving the performance you so want (see box).

So how can we prepare ourselves for combating race day nerves or for too much competitive anxiety?

Good concentration is about being totally absorbed.

Once you accept failure, you can achieve anything.

Controlling Competitive Anxiety and Nervous Tension

Fear of Failure Versus Need for Success

Once you accept failure, you can achieve anything. Fear of failure and the need for success can be a root cause of your anxiety. People who are really afraid of performing badly just won't compete. At the other end of this scale, if someone doesn't care at all, then why bother to perform? It is good to be somewhere in-between, probably around four to six on a ten point 'fear of failure' scale.

In a similar way, ask yourself how much you have a *need* for success. Do you depend on success for a certain amount of happiness? It might be that it is important for you to perform well to please your parents, coach or peers. Being over-dependent on success will be a distraction and cause too much anxiety. To combat

this, it is useful to think through your goals. Are they yours? Are they realistic? Are they performance-based, rather than results-based? Put orienteering success into perspective with the rest of your life and learn some strategies to control anxiety.

Nervous Tension

We are aiming for a relaxed nervous tension, as we need to be excited about the prospect of running well, but not so anxious that we can't think straight. Setting goals and preparing well will set us up to make sure some adrenaline is running on race day, but it is necessary to have some strategies to prevent going over the top and as a result losing energy and concentration through being over-anxious about a result.

From the time you wake up, focus your thoughts on how you are going orienteer. Try not to go down the road of picturing yourself standing on the rostrum with a medal round your neck, or getting loads of adulation from parents and friends. You may want these things, but they will only come if you orienteer well. If you think about them too much, you may make yourself too anxious. Your aim is to be nervous, but in control.

Negative and Positive Thoughts

If necessary, try to steer any negative thoughts away – let them go – and replace them with positive ones, such as

'I am going to find the first control first time by setting off steady and calm.' It is quite normal to find yourself thinking about winning or beating someone or making mistakes, but these mental images divert the focus from the task in hand – how you are going to orienteer. 'Letting

---

WAYS OF HELPING YOURSELF REMAIN CALM

Try these ways to keep calm:

- three to five deep breaths to relax
- sitting quietly away from others
- talking to people
- talking to yourself
- being active – warming up
- visualizing yourself orienteering well
- smiling and reminding yourself it is all supposed to be enjoyable.

Try not to always go down the road of picturing yourself with a medal round your neck.

SOME SYMPTOMS OF ANXIETY

These are some of the symptoms of anxiety:

- high resting heart rate
- sweaty palms
- 'butterflies' in the stomach
- nausea
- loss of appetite
- trembling hands
- headache
- needing the loo
- unable to focus clearly.

Smile and remind yourself it is all supposed to be enjoyable.

them go' is like letting an image disappear into the darkness, or just letting it fade away as you replace it with a sharp, positive image linked with performing. Some orienteers will find a quiet spot near the start, relax and do some positive visualization or self-talk as part of their warm-up routine to help them keep in control of their nerves; others will extend their warm-up and keep active, rather than stop and think about things too much. You need to analyse how you feel, then act to prevent a negative impact on your performance.

Relaxation

There is a technique to relaxation that is useful to know for any of life's anxious or stressful situations. Any sort of visualization has greater benefits if you do it when you are physically and mentally relaxed.

Start with three to five deep breaths. By taking in more oxygen into the lungs, the heart rate starts to slow down and more oxygen goes to the brain to help you think clearly. Once you have settled, systematically work up your body from your toes; tense up each muscle group as tight as you can, then completely let it relax and allow the tightness to drain away. You can tense up with an in-breath and relax with an out-breath. Don't forget to include buttocks, fingers and facial muscles.

However, if you are a person who is over-relaxed and could do with more nervous tension, the easiest way to create this is to breathe out fast and rapidly. Some aggressive running will also raise your heart rate. You could also think about some part of the race that will make you more excited. This could be a big prize, or something that will make you determined to run hard and orienteer well.

Racing Mantras and Trigger Words

Many orienteers talk to themselves whilst they are racing – honestly! The talking can be out loud or silent. This can be to reinforce decisions or follow a route. It also helps to keep focused on what you are doing and avoid being distracted.

Another technique to bring your concentration back from a distraction is to have a mantra or a trigger word that you repeat over again. It is like having your coach

---

RACING MANTRAS AND TRIGGER WORDS

Some orienteering mantras or trigger words:

- map
- focus
- concentrate
- control
- plan
- three–two–one
- T-CUP (Think Clearly Under Pressure)
- get a grip
- don't be silly.

---

telling you to 'get a grip' and get on with it, but you tell yourself. Mantras can be used before the start, as well as during a race.

Visualization and Mental Rehearsal

Orienteering is one of many sports that are very visual. You study the map, visualize how the landscape will look and run into it. If you are, say, a gymnast or slalom skier, a lot of visualization practice consists of seeing and feeling the body performing twists and turns perfectly in time, but as an orienteer you don't know exactly what the forest, each leg or control will look like, but you can imagine it. You know what sort of terrain you will be competing in, the type of race it is and how you want to perform.

This gives you plenty of material to set up some visualization sessions before your big races. Do some at home in the

Visualize yourself orienteering well. The clearer and sharper you can make your images, the better they are remembered.

VISUALIZATION

Some pictures for visualization:

- starting the race focused and calm
- seeing the map and route to the first control clearly
- running fluently and fast through the terrain; detail this picture with using the compass, thumbing the map and the feeling of confidence of knowing where you are all the time
- finding controls with good rhythm and flow
- focusing well towards the end of a race when you are tired.

---

so on.' Again, like the visualization, the more detail about *how* you orienteer, the better. Try it; it might feel odd, but it can work – if you believe it will. Don't just save this for the day before you race, when you are starting to get a bit nervous. Write it in as part of the pre-competition phase. Repeat it whenever you have an opportunity – at least three times a day. You could do this on a run or when you get into bed at night, it doesn't matter when. Try it.

In the days when I was orienteering for Great Britain, when few people believed the British could beat the Scandinavians on their home terrain, I helped myself overcome this by making myself a tape/CD telling myself how capable I was and how I

could orienteer just as well in Norway, Sweden or Finland as I could in this country. Then I played this in the car on the way to work, or travelling long distances. It might not suit everyone, but it helped me.

Before your next event, set yourself a goal you can achieve. Prepare as well as you can for it and believe you can have a good performance. Warm up well and spend a few minutes focusing on how you are going to orienteer. Do a little visualization, or just think about it while you are waiting in the pre-start area. Concentrate on orienteering at your best all the time you are out on the course. Finally, smile and enjoy yourself! Smiling helps you to relax and orienteering, of course, is such a great sport.

weeks before and also before the start. The more relaxed you are, the better your visualization. As you relax, try to bring in detail of the terrain and colours. What can you smell? What do you feel? The clearer and sharper you can make your imaginary pictures, the better they are absorbed and remembered by the body and mind. It might help to use a course you have run before in similar terrain to bring up clear pictures to visualize, then transfer these images into the race for which you are preparing.

Self-Talk

Don't be shy! Look in the mirror and tell yourself what a brilliant orienteer you are. This is not easy for most of us, but if self-belief is part of achieving your goals, then verbalizing it endorses what you believe or want to believe. This is a very personal process, which you may choose not to share with anyone else. Imagine you have a mentor or fairy godmother who gives you wisdom and will tell you just what you are capable of: 'Carol, you are one of the best orienteers in the world. You know how to orienteer fast. You aren't distracted by other people, you are always concentrating well going into controls and you know that you excel at control flow.'

Write down a few lines similar to this: '*I am one of the best orienteers in the world; I know how to orienteer fast and*

At your next major event prepare as well as you can for it and believe you can have a good performance.

INTERNATIONAL CONTROL DESCRIPTION SYMBOLS

IOF Event Example			
M45, M50, W21			
5		7.6 km	210 m

▷			╱	╱╲	╲Y	
1	101		⋰			‹
2	212	╲	▲		1.0	○·
3	135		✳✳			⊡
4	246	╎╀╎	⊖			◎
5	164	→	⸦⸧			·○
○ - - - - 120 m - - -›						
6	185		╱	⌐		⌐
7	178		⏍			∟○
8	147	±	⊓⊓		2.0	
9	149		╱	╱	×	
○ - - - - 250 m - - -›◎						

Control Descriptions for IOF Event Example
Classes M45, M50, W21

Course number 5		Length 7.6 km	Height climb 210 m
Start		Road, wall junction	
1	101	Narrow marsh bend	
2	212	North western boulder, 1 m high, east side	
3	135	Between thickets	
4	246	Middle depression, east part	
5	164	Eastern ruin, west side	
Follow taped route 120 m away from control			
6	185	Stone wall, ruined, south east corner (outside)	
7	178	Spur, north west foot	
8	147	Upper cliff, 2 m high	
9	149	Path crossing	
Follow taped route 250 m from last control to finish			

Sample control description sheet

These are in the order in which they are to be visited, and may incorporate special instructions such as the length and nature of any marked route during the course. A thicker horizontal line should be used after every third description and on either side of any special instruction.

A B C D E F G H		A	Control number
		B	Control code
		C	Which of any similar feature
2 | 225 | ↘ | ⋰ | ▦ | 8x4 | ‹· | 🯅		D	Control feature
		E	Appearance
		F	Dimensions / Combinations
		G	Location of the control flag
		H	Other information

Description of individual controls

Symbol	Name	Description
↑	Northern	The more northern of two similar features, or the northern-most of several similar features.
↘	South Eastern	The more south eastern of two similar features, or the south-eastern-most of several similar features.
➡•	Upper	Where the control feature is directly above a similar feature.
•➡	Lower	Where the control feature is directly below a similar feature.
|•|	Middle	Where the control feature is the middle one of a number of similar features.

Column C: which of any similar feature

Symbol	Name	Description
⟯	Terrace	A level area on a slope.
⟯	Spur	A contour projection or "nose" rising from the surrounding ground.
∧	Re-entrant	A contour indentation; a valley; the opposite of a spur.
⌢⌢	Earth bank	An abrupt change in ground level which can clearly be distinguished from its surroundings.
⌣	Quarry	Gravel, sand or stone working in flat or inclined ground.
⊞	Earth wall	A narrow wall of earth projecting above the surrounding terrain; may be partially stone faced, usually man-made. Used with symbol 8.11 to indicate a ruined earth wall.
∧	Erosion gully	An erosion gully or trench, normally dry.
◈	Small erosion gully	A small erosion gully or trench, normally dry.
◯	Hill	A high point. Shown on the map with contour lines.
•	Knoll	A small obvious mound. Used with symbol 8.6 to indicate a rocky knoll.
)(	Saddle	The low point between two higher points.
⊖	Depression	A depression or hollow from which the ground rises on all sides. Shown on the map with contour lines.
∪	Small depression	A small, shallow, natural depression or hollow from which the ground rises on all sides.
∨	Pit	A pit or hole with distinct steep-sides. Usually man made. Used with symbol 8.6 to indicate a rocky pit.
∪∪∪	Broken ground	Clearly disturbed ground with features too small or too numerous to be mapped individually; including animal earths.
✳	Ant hill (termite mound)	The mound made by ants or termites.

Column D: the control feature

Symbol	Name	Description
⊓⊓⊓	Cliff, Rock face	A cliff or rock face. May be passable or impassable.
▲	Rock Pillar	A high, natural rock projection.
⅄	Cave	A hole in a rock face or hill side, often leading to underground workings.
▲	Boulder	A prominent free-standing block of rock or stone.
▲▲▲	Boulder field	An area covered by so many boulders that they cannot be individually mapped.
▲▲	Boulder cluster	A small distinct group of boulders so closely clustered together that they cannot be individually mapped.
⠿	Stony ground	An area covered with many small stones or rocks.
❋	Bare rock	A runnable area of rock with no earth or vegetation cover.
ⅠⅭ	Narrow passage	A gap between two cliffs or rock faces that face each other.

Rocks and boulders

Symbol	Name	Description
⊚	Lake	A large area of water, normally uncrossable.
∿∪	Pond	A small area of water.
∿∨	Waterhole	A water-filled pit or depression.
∿∿	River, Stream, Watercourse	A natural or artificial watercourse with either moving or standing water.
⋇	Minor water channel, Ditch	A natural or man made minor water channel which may contain water only intermittently.
⋰⋰	Narrow marsh	A narrow marsh or trickle of water, too narrow to be shown on the map with the marsh symbol.
≡	Marsh	A permanently wet area with marsh vegetation.
⊡	Firm ground in marsh	A non-marshy area within a marsh, or between two marshes.
◯∿	Well	A shaft containing water or a captive spring, clearly visible on the ground. Often with some form of man-made surround.
⌇	Spring	The source of a watercourse with a distinct outflow.
∿⊏⊐	Water tank, Water trough	A man made water container.

Marsh and water

Symbol	Name	Description
✕	Special item	If used, an explanation of its meaning must be supplied to competitors in the pre-race information.
◯	Special item	If used, an explanation of its meaning must be supplied to competitors in the pre-race information.

Special features

Symbol	Name	Description
	Road	A metalled/asphalt surfaced or dirt road, suitable for vehicles in normal weather conditions.
	Track / Path	A visible route made by people or animals. Tracks may be driven by rugged vehicles.
	Ride	A clearly visible linear break in the forest which does not have a distinct path along it.
	Bridge	A crossing point over a watercourse, or other linear feature.
	Power line	A power or telephone line, cableway or ski lift.
	Power line pylon	A support for power or telephone line, cableway or ski lift.
	Tunnel	A way under roads, railways, etc.
	Stone wall	A stone boundary wall or stone faced bank. Used with symbol 8.11 to indicate a ruined stone wall.
	Fence	A wire or wooden boundary. Used with symbol 8.11 to indicate a ruined fence.
	Crossing point	A way through or over a wall, fence, or pipeline, including a gate or stile.
	Building	A standing brick, wood or stone structure.
	Paved area	An area of hard standing used for parking or other purposes.
	Ruin	The remains of a building that has fallen down.
	Pipeline	A pipeline (gas, water, oil, etc.) above ground level.
	Tower	A tall metal, wooden or brick structure, usually built for forest observation.
	Shooting platform	A structure attached to a tree where a marksman or observer can sit.
	Boundary stone, Cairn	A man made stone or pile of stones. A cairn, memorial stone, boundary stone or trigonometric point.
	Fodder rack	A construction for holding feed for animals.
	Charcoal burning ground	The clear remains of an area where charcoal was burned. A small level man made area on a slope. (A platform).
	Monument or Statue	A monument, memorial or statue.
	Building pass through	An arcade, indoor passage or route through a building.
	Stairway	A stairway of at least two steps.

Man-made features

Symbol	Name	Description
	Open land	An area with no trees. Grassland, a meadow or a field. Also heath or moorland.
	Semi-open land	An area of open land with scattered trees or bushes.
	Forest corner	The corner or tip of a forested area projecting into open land.
	Clearing	A small area of land free from trees within the forest.
	Thicket	A small area of forest where the tree cover or undergrowth is so dense that it is difficult to pass.
	Linear thicket	A man-made line of trees or bushes that is difficult to cross.
	Vegetation boundary	A distinct boundary between different types of trees or vegetation.
	Copse	A small area of trees in open ground.
	Distinctive tree	An unusual or distinctive tree in either open land or forest; frequently information is also given as to its type.
	Tree stump, Root stock	The stump of a tree. The upturned root of a fallen tree, with or without the trunk.

Vegetation

Symbol	Name	Description
	Low	Where the control feature is particularly low or flat but this is not indicated on the map; e.g. Hill, low.
	Shallow	Where the control feature is particularly shallow but this is not indicated on the map; e.g. Re-entrant, shallow.
	Deep	Where the control feature is particularly deep but this is not indicated on the map; e.g. Pit, deep.
	Overgrown	Where the feature is partially covered in undergrowth or bushes that are not indicated on the map; e.g. Ruin, overgrown.
	Open	Where the feature is in an area where the tree cover is less than the surroundings but this is not indicated on the map; e.g. Marsh, open.
	Rocky, Stony	Where the feature is in an area of rocky or stony ground not indicated on the map; e.g. Pit, rocky.
	Marshy	Where the feature is in an area of marshy ground not indicated on the map; e.g. Re-entrant, marshy.
	Sandy	Where the feature is in an area of sandy ground not indicated on the map; e.g. Spur, sandy.
	Needle leaved	Where the tree or trees associated with the control feature have needle shaped leaves; e.g. Distinctive tree, needle leaved.
	Broad leaved	Where the tree or trees associated with the control feature are broad-leaved; e.g. Copse, broad leaved.
	Ruined	Where the feature has fallen to ground level; e.g. Fence, ruined.

Column E: appearance

Dimensions

Symbol	Name	Description
2.5	Height or Depth	Height or Depth of the feature in metres.
8 x 4	Size	Horizontal dimensions of the feature in metres.
0.5/ /3.0	Height on slope	Height of the feature on a slope in metres.
2.0 3.0	Heights of two features	Heights of two features with the control between them.

Combinations

Symbol	Name	Description
X	Crossing	The point at which two linear features cross.
Y	Junction	The point at which two linear features meet.

When either of these symbols are used in Column F the two features which either cross or meet must be shown in columns D and E. For example:

D	E	F		
/	/	X	Path crossing	The point at which two similar linear features cross.
⋮	∿	X	Ride / River crossing	The point at which two different linear features cross.
/	/	Y	Road junction	The point at which two similar linear features meet.
∿	⋮	Y	River / Narrow marsh junction	The point at which two different linear features meet.

Column F: dimensions/combinations

Symbol	Name	Description
◌	North east Side	Used where the feature extends above the surface of the ground; e.g. Boulder, north east side; Ruin, west side.
⊋	South east Edge	Used where: a) The feature extends down from the surface of the surrounding ground and the control is situated on the edge at ground level; e.g. Depression, south east edge. b) The feature extends over a significant area and the control is situated on the border of that area; e.g. Marsh, west edge; Clearing, north west edge.
⊙	West Part	Used where the feature extends over a significant area and the control is located neither at the centre, nor on any of the edges; e.g. Marsh, west part; Depression, south east part.
⟩	East Corner (inside)	Used where: a) The edge of a feature turns through an angle of 45-135 degrees; e.g. Open land, east corner (inside); Ruin, north west corner (outside). b) A linear feature turns a corner; e.g. Fence, south corner (inside); Stone wall, south west corner (outside).
⋎	South Corner (outside)	The orientation of the symbol indicates the direction in which the corner points.
⋰	South west Tip	Used where the edge of a feature turns through an angle of less than 45 degrees; e.g. Marsh, south west tip.
<	Bend	Used where a linear feature makes a smooth change of direction; e.g. Path bend; River bend.
⟍	North west End	The point at which a linear feature ends or starts; e.g. Ride, north west end; Stone wall, south end.
⫼	Upper Part	Where the feature extends over two or more contours and the control is located near the top; e.g. Erosion Gully, upper part.
⫼	Lower Part	Where the feature extends over two or more contours and the control is located near the bottom; e.g. Re-entrant, lower part.
⋒	Top	Where the control is located at the highest point of the feature and this is not the usual location; e.g. Cliff, top.
⌐·⌐	Beneath	Where the control is located underneath the feature; e.g. Pipeline, beneath.
⌊	Foot (no direction)	Where the control is located at the lower junction of the slope of the feature and the surface of the surrounding area; e.g. Earth bank, foot.
◌ᴸ	North east Foot	As above, but where the feature is large enough for the control to be placed in more than one location around it; e.g. Hill, north east foot.
⊤	Between	Where the control is located between two features; e.g. Between thickets; Between boulder and knoll.

D	E	F	G		
※	※		⊤	Between thickets	The point between two similar features.
▲	●		⊤	Between boulder and knoll	The point between two different features.

Column G: location of the control flag

Symbol	Name/Description
⊙--- 60 m ---→	Follow Taped Route, 60m away from control.
⊙--- 300 m ---→⊙	Follow Taped Route, 300m between controls.

Symbol	Name/Description
⊗ ⊃⊂ ⊗	Mandatory crossing point or points.
⊗ ▭ ⊗	Mandatory passage through out of bounds area.

Symbol	Name/Description
⊙--- 50 m ---→△	Follow Taped Route, 50m to Map Exchange.

Symbol	Name/Description
⊙--- 400 m ---→⊙	400m from last control to Finish. Follow taped route.
⊙>-- 150 m ---→⊙	150m from last control to Finish. Navigate to finish funnel, then follow tapes.
⊗ 380 m ⊗	380m from last control to Finish. Navigate to finish. No tapes.

Symbol	Name	Description
✚	First aid post	Control site where First aid is available.
⛟	Refreshment point	Control site where Refreshments are available.
⚡	Radio or TV control	Location of a Radio or TV control.
大	Control check	Manned control site where the control card is checked.

Column H: other information

GLOSSARY

aiming off this is a safe and time-saving navigation technique to find a point on a line or long feature. It involves deliberately aiming to one side of the control so that you know which way to turn on hitting the feature before seeing the control.

attack point an obvious or easily found feature close to a control point. It is used in selecting and executing a route so that the control can be more easily located or 'attacked'.

bearing the direction of travel shown by the compass.

BOF British Orienteering Federation.

bramble bashers high knee socks with a protective rubber facing.

cartography map drawing.

catching feature an obvious feature on the map and ground beyond a control, which can be used for relocation if the control is missed.

clip compass a simple compass which clips onto the side of the map, allowing easy map orientation to north.

collecting feature a long or large feature, which can be used to simplify navigation along a route.

colour-coded system used for events where colours represent different technical levels and courses.

contact map contact is a term used for relating the ground to the map or the map to the ground, so that the orienteer knows where he or she is.

contour-only maps copies of maps with only the brown print, showing land form only and no other detail. A good training resource.

control (point) the points that must be visited in order to complete a course. Shown as a red and white kite in the terrain and the centre of a red circle on the map.

control card this is carried by the orienteer when pin punches are used at controls. The orienteer clips or punches their card in the correct numbered box to prove that they have visited each control on their course.

control code identification numbers that are displayed at each control. Code numbers are included on the description list to enable competitors to check that they have arrived at the correct control.

control descriptions every course has a list of control descriptions giving the order, the code numbers and features where each control is placed.

control flow an expression used for the fluency of arriving at, registering and moving away from a control point. Top orienteers will take 2–4sec to do this.

corridor a narrow band of map and terrain linking controls.

course a sequence of control points marked on the map and ground, which have to be visited in a given order. There will be different courses for different standards and age groups.

dog-leg positioning of a control that allows competitors to go in and leave by the same route, thereby leading other competitors to it.

electronic punching SI and Emit are two systems used in the UK for recording timed visits to controls. Competitors carry a 'dibber' or 'brick', which carries all the recorded times.

elite the top class at Championships. Competitors usually have to justify their ability and might be seeded with start times.

fartlek a Swedish word (meaning speed play) used to describe a running training session over a variety of paths and terrain with impromptu fast and slow sections.

fight impenetrable forest shown as dark green on an orienteering map.

fine orienteering precise navigation in detailed terrain, usually demanding careful use of map, compass and distance judgement. Recommended between attack point and control.

following cheating, except when being used non-competitively.

form line an intermediate or extra contour line showing ground detail to help the orienteer maintain map contact. They are shown as broken brown lines.

GPS Ground Positioning System. Can be used at most orienteering races to track routes, then linked with electronic race analysis systems.

handrail a line or long feature on the map and ground used by the orienteer to make his route safe and to simplify the map reading.

index contour every fifth contour line is drawn heavier to make the height and shape of the ground more obvious on the map.

knoll a small hill symbolized by a brown dot on the map.

leg the section of a course between two control points.

legend or **key** a list of symbols represented on the map with their meanings.

line course a training exercise where orienteers follow on the ground a line drawn on the map.

line features linear features on the map and in the terrain, for example paths, walls streams and so on.

locate when an orienteer uses the map and the surrounding features to find out where he or she is. See also 'relocate'.

M an abbreviation for men's age classes (H on the continent), for example M15 (boys aged fourteen and fifteen).

magnetic north lines shown on all orienteering maps so that the compass can be used accurately and bearings can be taken without having to add any degrees. Magnetic north is slightly west of true north and grid north.

map memory a course or controls where the orienteer does not have a map and has to memorize the legs from a map section displayed at base or at each control point.

master maps these are maps that show the course for each competitor to copy onto their own map. An outdated system superseded by pre-marked maps produced by OCAD and cheaper colour printing.

OCAD Orienteering Computer Aided Design. Computer software for drawing maps and setting courses.

orienting a map matching map to terrain so that north on the map points to north on the ground and the map matches the ground. Sometimes called 'setting the map'.

pace counting a system of counting double paces to check off distance covered over the ground.

permanent course a course set up with permanent marker posts and pre-marked maps for recreational use.

photogrammetry the use of air photographs for surveying maps. Photogrammetric base maps are drawn from air photographs in a stereo plotting machine by a skilled operator.

pre-marked map a map with the course overprinted that is normally given out to the competitor at the start.

pre-start personal call-up time at an event, usually 1–3min before the start time.

protractor compass the conventional compass with a rotatable housing and long base plate to enable bearings to be taken. The angle between direction of travel and north is measured and then followed.

punch a pin punch found at control points for competitors to mark their

control card to prove they have been to the control. Each control would have a punch with a different pattern of pins. Universally used before electronic checking came into use.

re-entrant a small valley shown by one or more contour lines.

relocation the orienteer tries to find their position when lost.

ride a clearly visible grassy or rough linear gap in the forest. A fire break would be shown as a wide ride.

rough compass running on a compass bearing or 'on the needle' without being too precise in keeping to the line of travel.

rough orienteering the orienteer runs fast on easy sections of a course, using rough compass and 'collecting' the major features along the route.

RouteGadget software for route analysis licensed to orienteering clubs.

runability a description of terrain in terms of how easy it is to run through. It is classified on the map by different colour screens.

score orienteering a competition to find as many controls as possible in any order, in a fixed time and with penalties for being late.

shadowing a training method of following an orienteer to watch how they perform skills and techniques in the forest. Often done by pairs exchanging roles.

simplification breaking down the route choice and navigation on each course leg into easy and difficult sections with the aid of check points, collecting features and attack points.

star exercise a training activity with start and finish at a central base. The participants visit one control at a time and then return to base before going on to the next one.

step system a progression of orienteering skills. It forms the basis of coaching, colour-coded competitions and the five technical levels of difficulty.

straight line route this is the shortest route between control points, but not always the fastest choice.

string courses short courses for very young children marked in the terrain by a continuous flagged route or string. Children find controls without getting lost. Controls are often fun animals or characters and the map simplified for easy understanding.

tags contour 'tags' are short brown lines used to show the downhill side of a contour line in areas where this might be confusing.

TD Technical Difficulty. Graded 1 to 5 and linked with colours.

thumb compass a compass which is fastened to the thumb of the orienteer's map hand, allowing easy map orientation and direction finding.

thumbing the orienteer holds the map with the thumb close to their location. The thumb moves as the orienteer progresses, enabling map contact to be kept along the chosen route.

vegetation boundary the line between two distinct types of vegetation shown by a black dotted line on maps, for example young trees and mature trees, or open and wooded.

W an abbreviation for women's age classes (D on the continent), for example W35 (women aged thirty-five to thirty-nine).

walk forest an area of dense woodland where running speed is much reduced.

wayfaring a rather dated term for non-competitive orienteering for groups or individuals.

USEFUL CONTACTS

UK Orienteering

British Orienteering

British Orienteering
8a Stancliffe House
Whitworth Road
Darley Dale
Matlock
DE4 2HJ
Tel: 01629 734042
Email: info@britishorienteering.org.uk
Web: www.britishorienteering.org.uk

The British Schools Orienteering Association

This exists to promote and develop all forms of Schools Orienteering, including participation in mainstream competitive sport. It provides discounted orienteering equipment, access to a network of regional contacts for advice in starting and developing orienteering within schools, as well as advice and information on coaching courses.

BSOA Marketing and Information Officer
55 Bruce Road
Kidderminster
DY10 2TY
Tel: 01562 631 561
Email: info@bsoa.org
Web: www.bsoa.org

eXplorer Challenge Award Scheme

A flexible and adaptable award scheme designed to encourage young people, by using maps, to venture into the outdoor world. Participants locate checkpoints, then receive badges and/or certificates. The award can be used on school sites and is very simple to administer.
Email: info@explorerchallenge.com
Web: www.bsoa.org

Books

Braggins, A., *Trail Orienteering* (British Orienteering, 1995)
McNeill, C., Cory-Wright, J. and Renfrew, T., *Teaching Orienteering* (Harvey, 1997)
McNeill, C. and Renfrew, T., *Start Orienteering*, a series of five books for teachers (Harvey, 2003)
McNeill, C. and Roberts, G., *Orienteering in Schools & Outdoor Centres* (Harvey, 2009)

Compass Sport – the magazine for orienteers.
Web: www.compasssport.com

Websites

Orienteering

English Orienteering – www.orienteeringengland.org.uk
Scottish Orienteering – www.scottish-orienteering.org
Welsh Orienteering – www.woa.org.uk
Northern Ireland Orienteering – www.niorienteering.org.uk/NIOA
International Orienteering Federation – www.orienteering.org and www.bmbo.org.uk
British Schools Orienteering Association – www.bsoa.org

Linked Sports

Trail Orienteering – www.trailo.org and www.orienteering.org
Mountain Bike Orienteering – www.orienteering.org and www.bmbo.org.uk
Ski Orienteering – www.orienteering.org
Le Trec – www.trec-uk.com – navigation on horseback

Clothing and Equipment

Compass Point orienteering shop
www.compasspoint-online.co.uk
Ultrasport orienteering shop
www.ultrasport.co.uk

Electronic punching equipment
www.sportident.com and www.emituk.com

News, Features, Forums

www.nopesport.com
www.worldofo.com

Training

www.attackpoint.org
www.brianmac.co.uk

Useful Applications for Training

GPS-enabled exercise log book software
www.zonefivesoftware.com/SportTracks

Results Analysis

www.routegadget.co.uk
www.splitsbrowser.org.uk
www.obasen.nu/winsplits/online/en

Orienteering Game

www.catchingfeatures.com

Course Planning Software

www.condes.net
www.ocad.com
www.purplepen.golde.org

Miscellaneous Useful and Interesting Sites

www.oobrien.com/map
www.maprunner.co.uk
www.tero.fr
www.simattu.ch/home

INDEX